HOW TO GET LAID

THE GAY MAN'S ESSENTIAL GUIDE TO HOT SEX

HOW TO GET LAID
THE GAY MAN'S ESSENTIAL GUIDE TO HOT SEX

JONATHAN BASS

alyson books
los angeles

Celebrating Twenty-Five Years

Manufactured in the United States of America.

This trade paperback original is published by Alyson Books,
P.O. Box 4371, Los Angeles, California 90078-4371.
Distribution in the United Kingdom by Turnaround Publisher Services Ltd.,
Unit 3, Olympia Trading Estate, Coburg Road, Wood Green,
London N22 6TZ England.

First edition: June 2005

05 06 07 08 09 a 10 9 8 7 6 5 4 3 2 1

ISBN 1-55583-886-3
ISBN-13 978-1-55583-886-7

Library of Congress Cataloging-in-Publication Data
   Bass, Jonathan, 1974–
      How to get laid : the gay men's essential guide to hot sex / Jonathan
   Bass.—1st ed.
      ISBN 1-55583-886-3; ISBN-13 978-1-55583-886-7
      1. Sex instruction for gay men. 2. Gay men—Sexual behavior. 3. Gay
   men—Social life and customs. I. Title.
   HQ76.1 .B37 2005
   306.76'62—DC22   2005045299

Cover art and design by Amy Martin.
Author illustration by Glen Hanson.

CONTENTS

Introduction 1

One:	The Male Sex Drive	5
Two:	How to Get Laid	13
Three:	Where the Boys Are	37
Four:	Deciding What You Really Want in Bed	61
Five:	A Safe Bet	82
Six:	Making the Best of Bad Situations	94
Seven:	The Morning After	118
Eight:	Sleeping Around Etiquette	128
Nine:	Nonmonogamy and Coming Out of a Relationship	137
Ten:	Are You a Stud or a Slut?	155

Glossary 158

INTRODUCTION

You think you know how to get laid? Sure, gay men can have sex on demand—it's our defining stereotype! You're confident enough, hot enough, and sexy enough to hook up whenever and wherever the mood strikes you, right?

Well, honey, I'm calling your bluff. You've played the field, made your conquests, and had one-night hookups—maybe even a regular fuckbuddy, a few threesomes, or an anonymous boy-bang at the local sex club. You're a walking, talking encyclopedia of homo sex info, and you don't need no stinking book to tell you how to score. Right? Bullshit.

The fact is that as crazy as we gay boys are for some hot loving, we've all had horrible lays. Maybe someone had too much to drink and couldn't get it up—or worse, maybe you *could* get it up, and only afterward, in the light of dawn when you first got a clear look at him, did you realize how thick your beer goggles had been. Maybe he claimed to be a total top stud in bed, but when you got him to your hotel room (and before you could even drop your pants), he was on all fours with his face buried in the pillow.

Or maybe you've got a nagging feeling that you're not sexy enough to get laid as often as you want to, or that you're not tall enough, or buff enough, or hung enough. I'm here to tell you otherwise.

I will show you how to develop the confidence to get laid. I will debunk the myths about gay sex. I'll teach you some irresistible come-on techniques, and I'll teach you what guys are really after—even if they're saying they're after something else.

In case you hadn't guessed by now, this book is not about how to get into a meaningful long-term relationship. Relationships are good. They can be great. Relationships can change your life for the better, and if you've never had one I'd definitely recommend one. But that's not why I'm here, and that's not why you're reading this book. Although this book might *help* get your gay *self* into bed with someone who's relationship material, this is emphatically not a "relationship" or "self-help" book.

So who is this book for?

This book is for you single gay/queer/SGL/bi men, and for you paired-up guys who like to play around with a third (or more) when the mood strikes you. This book is not for you monogamous types who claim never to have had a slut phase. (Liars.) This book is for any guy who is interested in the art of the hookup. This book is for you guys who need a little sexual healing—and who want more dick, and more ass, and more of the stuff that makes you howl like the wild man you are—in your life.

Knowing how to get laid is important. It's equally important to learn how to pick up the signals that will help you determine if your Mr. Right Now is going to be a good lay, or if he's going to be a pillow princess who makes you do all the work in bed. Is he going to want to stick around to watch the

Today Show with you in the morning (or are you going to want him out of your bed and out of your house before *The Late Show* comes on at night). I'll help you suss out all the secret signals you need to know and teach you how to make sure he doesn't stay for Katie Couric and coffee unless you really want him to.

You'll learn what he really means when he says he wants to "get together" again soon, and you'll know for sure whether you want to "get together" again or not. You'll learn to detect the games we homos play, and how to cut through the crap in a fraction of the time it used to take you.

So here's to learning the tricks of the trade, and to turning your tricks (and your trade) into hot, safe, memorable lays...happy reading!

THE MALE SEX DRIVE

1

What's So Great About Sex?

Men are crazy for sex. As gay men we go to extraordinary lengths—shelling out big money on dates, spending hours and hours at the gym, modifying our body hair, piercing some of our body parts, tattooing other parts, buying new wardrobes, and more—all in the pursuit of booty. But why? What is so compelling about sex?

Is it because of the way it feels to have sex or to be aroused? The experiences of arousal and sexual fulfillment are like a drug, one we turn to over and over again for a fix—and they can be all-consuming if we let them. A bad case of the hornies can put blinders on the best of us, so that all we can see or think about is sex. The cock wants what it wants, and we're often all too happy to help it pursue its earthly goals.

Clearly sex is too powerful to ignore. Ask an adult who is celibate (by choice) how difficult it is to refrain from sex. It's tough. Sexual desire can set you aflame, or make your body feel positively electric, charging your skin as though a current were running through it. Getting off and getting aroused produces such a natural high—it's the stuff of poetry, music, books, and movies. How much art has been created in the name of wooing someone for sex? (Probably lots, but since I don't have the statistics on that, let's just move on.)

The orgasm is the perfect drug, and sex is the most effective escape into pure pleasure. Have you ever worried about your overdue phone bill or the Middle East crisis when you were coming? I didn't think so.

What's Going On Down There?

Our bodies seem to know that sex is important. The physiological explanation for our pursuit of cock, in a nutshell, is this: You can blame it on your balls. If you've got balls, you're making testosterone—the most important male sex hormone—and you're getting between four and 10 milligrams a day from your testicles and your adrenal glands. In men, testosterone stimulates the growth of bone and muscle, the enlargement of the genitals and testicles, the development of the male secondary sex characteristics that occur at puberty (armpit and pubic hair), and the maintenance of muscle bulk. Testosterone will make you really horny too, and testosterone maintains the plumbing in your dick to get it hard and keep it up when you're aroused.

OK, so testosterone makes us horny. But is there a reason we need to be horny? The prevailing biological explanation is that men are driven on a fundamental survival-of-the-species level to assure that their genetic code is passed on to as many offspring as possible. Naturally, being horny facilitates the passing on of the genetic code: The more one acts on his horniness by having sex, the more seed he spreads around.

But as gay men, we're more often playing hide the sausage

with other male members of the species, not with women. Men don't produce eggs to accept sperm, so when we fags spill our seed, there's no receptacle for our genetic code. In other words, our seed-spreading is nonprocreative. Because of that, some religious types and other cultural commentators theorize that we're the ultimate sex fiends—indiscriminately spreading seed far and wide without making babies. (Or maybe we're just more evolved...)

So it's a biological imperative to spread our seed? Try as I might, I've never gotten one man pregnant. Thank God! Can you imagine how many babies we'd have in this world if gay men could impregnate one another? Nevertheless, if a biological imperative to procreate is at work in the male sex drive, I've gotten along just fine without procreating.

The point for us gay guys is that, even while you're sitting here reading this book, your body is manufacturing testosterone and sperm. *Lots* of sperm, and at an alarming rate. You're not alone—we're all doing it. Every time you pop a load, you're releasing a few hundred *million* sperm. Think about that next time you toss that used tissue into the trash.

There are also sociological reasons for our sex drive. This is still, by many standards, a man's world. Masculinity and power are equated with one another, and virility is linked with masculinity in the minds of people throughout the world. We're told in many different ways—especially through TV and movies and other forms of mass media—that sexual prowess is one of the most clearly identifiable ways for a man to demonstrate masculinity, assert his power, and secure his social standing. So, in other words, if you are getting some, you're a real man. We're socialized to demonstrate our power through sex. We're told that if you're not getting sex, you're not a complete man. To be impotent, sexless, or androgynous is to be powerless. To want sex is to be virile, masculine, powerful.

The True Cost of Sex

But does all the above really account for the time, money, and effort we put into getting laid? Sex can last from a few minutes to a few hours. But even if it lasts a respectable 30 minutes to an hour each time, that's a relatively small portion of your day—or of your week if you're not having sex daily.

Is 30 minutes of fun worth it? Here, in dollars and cents, is a breakdown of the true cost of getting laid in a variety of scenarios and locales.

The Cost of Sex: Bar or Dance Club

Variables include your appetite for liquor and for bar games (pool, darts, etc.), the night of the week (which determines cover charge), the relative cost of the drinks you buy, transportation, and whether you purchase drinks for a prospective lay.

Cover charge	none-$20
Cocktails/beer	$20-50
Drink for him (1-2)	$10-15
Pool, pinball, darts	$5
Transportation (gas and parking/subway)	$5
Condoms	$7
Lube (midsize bottle)	$16
Total	$63-118

The Cost of Sex: Dinner Date

Variables include your appetite for expensive wine, whether either of you is on a no-carb (and hence, no dessert) diet, and relative cost of restaurant.

```
Appetizers . . . . . . . . . . . . . . . . . . . . . . . . .$7-20
Entrées for two . . . . . . . . . . . . . . . . . . . . . .$20-50
Wine/cocktails/beverages . . . . . . . . . . . . . . .$20-50
Dessert . . . . . . . . . . . . . . . . . . . . . . . . . . .$8-12
Tip (20% to impress him) . . . . . . . . . . . . . . . .$11-26
Transportation (gas, valet, parking) . . . . . . . . .$5-15
Condoms . . . . . . . . . . . . . . . . . . . . . . . . . .$7
Lube (midsize bottle) . . . . . . . . . . . . . . . . . .$16
Total . . . . . . . . . . . . . . . . . . . . . . . . . . . . .$94-196
```

The Cost of Sex: Online Date

Does not include purchase price of computer

```
Internet service provider/cable/DSL (per month) . .$20-60
Condoms . . . . . . . . . . . . . . . . . . . . . . . . . .$7
Lube (midsize bottle) . . . . . . . . . . . . . . . . . .$16
Total . . . . . . . . . . . . . . . . . . . . . . . . . . . . .$43-83
```

The Cost of Sex: Solo Date

All items are optional.

```
Porn magazine . . . . . . . . . . . . . . . . . . . . . . .$4-6
Dirty movie rental . . . . . . . . . . . . . . . . . . . . .$3-6
Sex toy . . . . . . . . . . . . . . . . . . . . . . . . . . . .$15-70
Lube (midsize bottle) . . . . . . . . . . . . . . . . . .$16
Cheapo lube substitute (hand lotion) . . . . . . . . .$3
Imagination . . . . . . . . . . . . . . . . . . . . . . . . .priceless
Total . . . . . . . . . . . . . . . . . . . . . . . . . . . . .$3-98
```

Time Keeps on Ticking

A simple solo date between your dick and your hand can

cost as little as three bucks, but a hookup with another person starts out at $43 bucks for a few online sessions. A dinner date can set you back as much as $200 (assuming you stay away from the TGI-McHooligan's chain restaurants) or more if you have expensive tastes. But to simply count the cost in dollars is to say nothing of your time commitment. We spend time exercising to keep us looking and feeling fit. We spend time selecting a wardrobe that's stylish and comfortable. We spend time showering, shaving, plucking the monobrow, and washing behind our ears. We spend time cleaning our dens of iniquity so that when we bring a date back to our place and we're bumping uglies, we're not knocking over stacks of dirty laundry. To sum it all up: Fucking takes time.

Take a look at the real cost, in hours, of getting some hot homo action:

Sex Time: Preparation for Dating

Gym/exercise . . . . .2.25-6.0 hours per week
Selecting suitable attire . . . . . . .0.5-1.0 hours per date
Grooming . . . . .0.5-1.0 hours per date*
Cleaning house/apartment . . . . . .1.0-3.5 hours per date
Total .4.25-11.5 hours per date

Assuming one date per week, that's up to 10.5 hours per date. (*And actors and models can easily triple or quadruple their mirror time.)

Sex is Good for You

Ultimately, it's obvious that we do feel that getting some action is worth the time, money, and hassle. Sex feels fantastic. If that weren't enough, scientific evidence is accumulating to support what many of us have suspected all along: Good sex not only adds great enjoyment to our lives but also improves our health and may even contribute to our longevity. Regular, enthusiastic sex has plenty of health benefits associated with it. The benefits include:

• *An improved sense of smell*—After bumping uglies, your body's production of the hormone prolactin increases. Prolactin causes stem cells in your brain to create new neurons in your olfactory bulb, where you process information about smells.

• *Lowered risk of heart disease*—Having sex three or more times a week cuts men's risk of stroke and heart attack in half.

• *Fitness levels increase*—Sex burns calories. An enthusiastic romp can burn up to 200 calories or so, about the same as 30 minutes on a treadmill. Plus, it's excellent exercise for your thighs, buttocks, arms, neck, and abs.

• *Pain and stress relief*—During orgasm, a naturally occurring chemical called oxytocin surges to as much as five times its normal level in your bloodstream. Endorphin levels shoot up as well, and that also alleviates pain. An orgasm is relaxing, helps you sleep, calms you down, and may reduce risk of stroke because it lowers your blood pressure. Oxytocin can also be helpful in healing wounds.

• *Fewer colds and flu*—Having sex at least once a week boosts your body's levels of an antibody called immunoglobulin A, which strengthens your immune system.

• *Reduced risk of prostate cancer*— A recent study published in *British Journal of Urology International* (not a riveting read, so just take my word for it) states that men can cut their chances of getting prostate cancer by one third if they ejaculate more than five times a week in their 20s.

Whatever your reason for getting it on—for your health, because the TV told you to, because it feels good—I'm here to help you get better sex more often. Getting laid isn't always easy work, but knowing a thing or two about how to get laid right (yes, there is a wrong way) will make it more enjoyable for you and for all the guys who will benefit from your attention.

2 HOW TO GET LAID

Here we are, at the heart of the matter. Once you've found your Moby Dick, you've got to have the hook and tackle to catch the big fish and reel him in. And this is where you will learn the skills that will make you a master with your rod. This chapter has the tips and tricks that will help you get more play with the boys.

Remember, these are not instructions on how to start or maintain a romantic relationship. If that's what you're looking for you've got the wrong book in your hands—and you don't read book covers very carefully apparently! This little tome is all about getting down and dirty. Granted, many a long-term relationship has started as a quickie in a mall bathroom or a randy rendezvous after a night of drinking, but if you're really in the market for an **LTR** (look for **bold** terms in the glossary), I'd suggest checking the self-help aisle of your local gay bookstore.

Through these guidelines, you'll learn how to detect your likes, dislikes, and weak spots as a gay man and turn them into hook-up techniques. But with newfound power comes newfound responsibility. With the insights you gain into the gay male libido, you must promise to use your powers only for good, never for evil.

While these tips range from things to say to ways to subconsciously suggest your intent through body language, the basic elements in this section involve getting into the mindset for your manhunt and learning what attracts and repels guys (just being a guy doesn't always clue you in).

Confidence

Confidence is the common denominator among guys who score when they're looking for sex. If you haven't got it, you haven't got much hope of getting what you want. Being the sort of cute-but-insecure-quirky-guy-with-a-heart-of-gold will get you laid if you're the protagonist in a gay indie film. But the real world is a harsher place, and a lack of confidence in a flesh-and-boner guy is about as appealing as a cold sore.

Hot guys without much confidence can be shy and self-effacing and still get some play because they're hot. Honestly, how many of us are truly drop-jaw need-a-fire-suit-you're-so-hot gorgeous? Only a few. Conversely, average-looking guys who have a level of confidence that borders on cocky are far more appealing than the average guys who are shy.

T.J., 30, a freelance writer in Los Angeles, says "Just think about Nicholas Cage. He's certainly not a conventionally attractive guy, and he's not really *ugly-hot* either. I mean, I'd never pick him out of a crowd. Yet he just comes off as hot when he's playing a cocksure guy on screen. And he's got that whole soft-spoken Elvis thing going on too. Confidence is definitely sexy. It can make an otherwise unattractive person exude an animal magnetism. Why do you think Angelina fell for Billy Bob? Because he was hot? Hell no!

"There's this guy I've known as an acquaintance for a while. He's not the studliest guy in town. He's got a crooked smile and a decent body, but it's not stunning. His hairline even recedes a little bit. But whenever I see him out he's always smiling and having a good time. He just acts like he knows he can get any guy he wants but he's not going to sweat it if he doesn't. He always has a few guys hanging on him because he's kind of cocky, and he's relaxed. His attitude is hot. I've gone home with him a couple of times just because his attitude is attractive."

As nice as it would be to pop a confidence pill or simply resolve to be surer of yourself, confidence is something that you usually have to develop gradually. But there are techniques that can get you around the normal confidence-learning curve to make you appear more confident in a hurry, even if you're not.

Let's take a lesson from the service industry. If you've ever worked in customer service or as a waiter or in a hotel—anyplace where a positive attitude affects your success—then you know that you have to smile for the customers even if you don't feel jubilant. Often people who do a lot of work over the phone are encouraged to smile, even if the customer cannot see them smiling. Smiling actually changes your voice in a way that is not immediately perceptible, but it's still conveyed to the customer on the other end of that phone line. Acting happy even if you're not has an impact on your demeanor and it can create a feedback loop: If you act pleasantly, customers will respond more positively to you, and that can make dealing with them a more pleasant experience. Bingo! Your day is looking up.

The same technique can be applied to our search for sex. Doing small things that represent poise and self-assurance can make people perceive you as more secure with yourself.

When people react well to your apparent level of confidence because you look relaxed and sure of yourself, you become more confident.

So how do we start acting like we're more confident? Here's an easy one: Slow down. Slow down your walk. Slow down your talk. Slow down your moves. Slow everything down. When you get nervous—like if you're talking to a hot guy at the deli counter at the supermarket—it's natural to speed up your speech and get tongue-tied. When we're nervous, we often get louder too. Loudness is often a cover-up for insecurity. The guys you're chatting up will instantly know you're tense, perceive your insecurity, and be turned off. So slow it down. When you're talking with that hot guy at the deli counter, slow it down just a bit. Measure your words carefully and don't get loud. Take a breath before you speak if you feel like you're going to rush through a sentence. Speaking more slowly will draw in anyone you're speaking with. And remember that a whisper is far sexier than a shout.

Shy, uncomfortable people hate to make an entrance. But you're not going to look shy or self-conscious when you slow down your moves too. Rather than rushing into a bar and quickly taking a chair in a corner or rushing into a movie theater before the lights go down and taking the first available seat, slow it down. You don't have to be flamboyant or flashy, but you should make an entrance. The goal is to enter a space with a quiet assertiveness that demonstrates that you own the room, you're in control of yourself, and you know you're attractive. Other people will stop and notice you. The more you feel that you own the space you inhabit, the more sex appeal you will radiate.

Move deliberately. Would James Bond rush when he didn't have to? Would Frank Sinatra raise his voice or get tongue-tied? You don't have to act exactly like Bond or Sinatra—just keep them in mind occasionally. If your actions look purposeful and deliberate rather than rushed, you'll appear more secure, and that will make you more attractive. The feedback loop will begin.

Making the Grade

Even where hot gay men are plentiful, the key to successfully getting laid is a numbers game. You have to expect to be shot down more often than you score. And knowing that the odds are against you will help you keep a healthy perspective on your goal.

You're going to increase your batting average with the tips in this chapter. Still, you will get shot down occasionally—maybe even often. We all get turned down. The idea is that knowing this will remind you that it's important to keep trying even when you're getting more no's than yes's.

I'll share the insights of my friend Shawn, 33, a graphic artist in New York. His idea should be taken with a large grain of salt (some of his math is "fuzzy," to borrow a political phrase), but the essence of the argument is worth listening to.

The Gay Bar Theorem goes like this: In any gay bar in the world where you'll find a good assortment of men, you can split the room into grades of attractiveness—like grading on a curve. The top 10% of the most attractive guys will appeal to nearly everyone in the bar. They get A's. They're the guys you would definitely go home with if they asked.

The next 20% along the curve are decent looking, and you'd very likely consider a hookup if they approached you. They're the B's and the C's. (The list goes to J's.) Whatever your relative eligibility in that environment, if you're in a cohort group (guys of similar age, etc.), then one in 10 of the men in the bar will be attracted to you as well because they'll be in a similar ranking—or grade. People tend to pair up with people who are roughly as attractive as they are, by societal standards. That means most of the A's will be interested only in other A's. Most of the B's will go for other B's, etc. You still have a chance with A's and B's even if you're a C or a D, but your success rate will be higher if you're talking to other C's and D's too. On average, if you talk to a dozen guys in a night, one or two of them will be interested.

Shawn is a self-described C who does pretty well hooking up. What he's getting at is that if you're only interested in A's—the most attractive guys in the room—then you're narrowing your options too much. The trick to improving your chances of hooking up is to talk not only to A's but to B's, C's, and even some D's, F's, and G's. ("I've had a couple of really fucking hot F's in my bed," Shawn remarks.) Some guys are much more attractive when you get a sense of their personality, and hot guys don't have a monopoly on hot sex. Save hitting on the A's for when you've had some practice with some of the more approachable guys.

Don't Swoop Too Soon

When you see a guy enter a party or club, don't rush up to put your moves on him as soon as he arrives. Arriving at a party or a club often entails saying hi to friends who might be there, ordering a cocktail, and getting a little comfortable. Give the object of your affection a minute to get his bearings. Guys who go out expect to meet several people over the course of the night, and they're unlikely to go home with the first man who says hi. You've got time.

Allow the cuties to acclimate and get a little comfortable first. And if someone beats you to the punch, don't sweat it just yet. If your competition pounced on the fox too soon, he's doomed to fail too. Observe, listen, and wait for the right moment to make your move.

Getting to Know Rejection

Ah, rejection. Bracing like a winter breeze, rejection can refresh and invigorate you... Oh, sorry, that's a peppermint patty.

Rejection pretty much sucks no matter how you look at it. It's about as fun as a paper cut and it can make you feel as pretty as an airport. (That means *way* not pretty, incidentally.)

But rejection happens to most guys at some point, so the trick is learning to not let it affect you for a long time. If you don't let it bother you, then you'll be ready to move on quickly. So flash your best smile, lean in close, talk low, and throw some killer Sinatra vibes his way. If he still won't take the bait, smile and be polite, even if he's not. Then move on.

Not all guys are looking for the same thing when it comes to hooking up. The guy who just rejected you may be in a monogamous relationship, or he may not be interested in a sexual relationship or a one-night stand. Or he may just not be interested in you. It happens. And you'll live through it.

The sooner you're comfortable approaching a guy with the knowledge that he might just turn you down—especially if that's the worst that could happen—the sooner you'll eliminate your fear of approaching guys. When your fear of rejection is gone, you'll be more confident—heck, you may even become invincible!

If your advances are rejected, take my friend Shawn's advice: "It's smart to chill out for a few minutes after you've been turned down before you try approaching another guy, especially in a bar or club where guy number 2 might have seen that you were talking with someone else first. The next guy you talk to won't appreciate being your second choice—and that's what he'll think he is if you come right over to him after being shot down. So pay attention to the other guys in the place, even if they're not exactly who you're after, because you'll want to know if they're looking at you. If your first choice guy says no thanks, maybe take a lap around the club or involve yourself in a non-hookup-oriented conversation with a friend. Then approach someone else after some decent downtime."

Regret is far more damaging than rejection. It's always better to be rejected than to wish you'd spoken with a hot guy, but your fear got the better of you and you never gave it a shot.

Think About Sex to Get Laid

You've probably heard the statistics that men think about

sex every eight minutes or every 15 seconds or whatever it is. Well, finally, it's going to come in handy.

When you're cozying up to a man you want to take home, envision the kind of hot, acrobatic, frenzied sex you want to have with him. Don't say anything about your mental gymnastic nastiness to him just yet—there will be time enough for that. This is for the small-talk portion of the getting-to-know-you session. Thinking about sex will subtly change the way your body moves, the tone of your voice, the position of your eyelids. (They call them bedroom eyes for a reason.)

Just thinking about slowly unbuttoning his jeans and slipping them down over his thick, hairy thighs will cause you to exude an unspoken sensuality. Picturing him bent over your couch will help too. Don't lose focus on what he's saying, but have a background porno playing in your head—with him in the starring role.

This train of thought will ever so slightly influence the signals you're sending out. Not only will these vibes convey an unspoken attraction that he'll pick up on, but they'll also help keep him from thinking of you as a "friend" candidate. You'll be dropping hints without even knowing exactly what you're doing it, and if he's conscious, he'll catch on.

Naked Alone Time

Many of the lessons in this chapter are based on the idea that confidence is sexy. One fundamental part of developing your confidence is to develop a body that looks and moves confidently. Keeping healthy and physically fit are musts for any guy, and they go a long way to make you appear self-assured. You don't need to go to the gym for hours a day sculpting mammoth pectorals, but working on keeping the muscles in your chest and back fit and toned will broaden shoulders and open your chest. Keeping your lower back and abdomen fit will improve your posture.

Another tip for developing a good body image is to spend some time alone in your birthday suit. A little naked alone time can do wonders for your confidence. Research has shown that being naked promotes a better body image. So unleash that inner go-go boy by stripping down and hanging out naked as much as you can. Take any opportunity you can to go au naturel—whether you're cleaning up around the house, or doing laundry, or reading the paper with a cup of coffee. Just watch that you don't spill!

Guys who are comfortable with their bodies aren't always perfectly fit gym gods. But guys with a good body image don't mind being naked, or partially clothed, whenever the situation requires. By getting naked (alone at first) you'll quickly see how your attitude toward your body and your sense of your own body image can change for the better.

You've done your housework naked; now you've got to go to bed naked. Sleeping in the nude is hardly scandalous, so if you've never tried it, give it a shot. If it's something you don't ordinarily do, you can start gradually, by going from pajamas the first night to underwear and a T-shirt the next, then just some briefs or boxers, then nude. The more time you spend without clothes, the better you'll feel about your body, and the boost to your confidence will happen a lot more quickly than you might think.

Pinpoint the Approachable

The next time you're in a gay bar, nightclub, GLBT organization meeting, or gayish coffee house, take a good look around the room. Why do some people look at ease and totally approachable, while others look put out and resistant to human interaction? Some guys have perfected the art of looking pissed-off or stuck-up. Sometimes it's intentional, and sometimes it's not. A chronic bad attitude can manifest itself in a number of ways, from a closed-off posture to a permanent grimace to a furrowed brow. Of course, some guys truly are pissed, while others have just been conditioned to use their grimaces as a shield—like loud talkers—to hide feelings of insecurity and inadequacy.

You can use your observations of the guys around you to your advantage in two ways:

First, make sure your body language is open and inviting. If other guys are looking closed off, don't do what they're doing. Ask yourself if you look approachable. If not, what can you do to make yourself appear more self-assured and inviting? Take a look at the body-language section in this chapter for more hints and tips.

Second, since no one else is approaching the guys with the bad attitude, maybe you should. If you see an attractive guy who looks put out, observe him carefully (without being noticed at first, if at all possible). Does he look mad or angry, or might he just be shy and not particularly good at masking it. Does he relax when he talks with his friends? He may not understand the signals he's giving off, so he might not actually be in a bad mood.

Santiago, 28, is a manager at a Los Angeles gourmet food market and a keen observer of mood: "If in the course of your observations, you determine that the guy you're into is truly in a bad mood, your odds of scoring are really low. If you approach him and he's not in the mood for a chat-up, he'll associate you with the bad mood and you'll probably never get to see him doing a naked spread eagle on your dining room table.

"But if you can tell he's the kind of guy who is just lousy at relating to other people, he may be really excited that you came up and said hi—because the other guys are turned off by his attitude. He might be an easy mark."

Body Language

Body language consists of the gestures, postures, and facial expressions by which we nonverbally express our states of mind. To the extent that we're interested in them here, they include the signals you and other guys give off to indicate a level of sexual interest or sexual availability.

Most of the time our body language is expressed without conscious thought. Knowing how to decipher a few key bits of body language will help you learn what other guys are thinking, even if they're saying otherwise. And knowing how to modify your own body language will help you send inviting signals. Here are some key body-language indicators that will help decode what guys are really thinking:

• Shy guys are often betrayed by a slouching posture, or by a habit of looking at their shoes when they're talking to a potential hookup. So lesson one is posture: shoulders back, tummy in, head up. Keep your hands out of your pockets (it indicates nervousness) and don't cross your arms over your chest (a defensive posture).

• Eye contact is the oldest gay cruising technique in the book—and one of the most reliable ways to determine the sexuality of a stranger (other than looking at his shoes). Men who are strangers tend not to look each other in the eye unless they're attracted to (or trying to intimidate) one another. Gay men maintain eye contact to indicate attraction. The classic gay cruise involves walking past a man while making eye contact with him, looking away, then slowing down and turning to see if he's looking back at you a second time. If he maintains that second gaze a bit longer, like three or four seconds, you're in. Most people avoid direct eye contact after a second or two, but if the man who interests you returns your gaze for

as long as you do—almost uncomfortably long—you can be fairly sure he wants to get to know you better. If you've made eye contact but he walks away from you, watch him for a few seconds more to see if he does something that indicates he might be a little nervous, like adjusting his clothing, looking distracted, or fidgeting. This means he knows you're watching, and though he's nervous, he's interested.

• When he starts telling you about where he got the shirt you remarked on (see Compliments), look him right in the eye, or on the mouth. Both are subconsciously arousing gestures.

• Don't chew your straw. Don't pull the label off your beer. Don't jingle the change in your pocket. Don't rattle your keys. Don't fidget—it will betray your nervousness. The attitude you want to project is calm, cool, and collected—not anxious, agitated, and apprehensive.

• Dilated pupils and increased blinking are signals of arousal.

Since you likely cannot dilate your pupils on command, and since increased blinking can't be done naturally, just look for those signals in guys you're getting close with. This changes as well with the level of light in a room, so see if you can tell whether his pupils shrink when he talks to someone else. Whether you can tell or not, looking in his eyes will indicate your interest.

• If your back is to him, turn your head—not your body—and smile at him. This cross-body look is a signal of interest.

• Body positioning is very important. When facing him, notice his shoulder orientation. If he's attracted to you, his upper body will be faced toward you. In essence, he'll aim his shoulders toward what he wants: you. If his feet or legs are spread somewhat, this means he's comfortable in his surroundings. If he leans into you (this one's an easy sign), he's attracted to you. Run with it!

• If he finds an excuse to touch you—like by touching your arm to make a point when he's telling you a story—this is a strong indication of attraction. You'll want to remember the story he's telling and ask him to retell it in the morning before you fuck again.

• If he laughs at your stories or jokes, you're in like Flynn. Don't start thinking you're all that funny though. We laugh at stupid shit when our cocks are in charge. Just take the hint and follow through. Don't go to open-mike comedy night.

• This one is a little experiment. If you get the sense that a guy is watching you, look at your watch for a count of three, then look at him. If he checks his watch too, then he's definitely watching you. We tend to copy the actions of someone we find attractive. (If he copies you, try going over and saying you noticed he was looking at this watch. Ask if he's planning to leave, and if he wants some company.)

Teamwork

Make your friends work for you when you're out and about. Friends can be real assets when you're hooking up, and you can be beneficial to them too.

Trey, 24, is an intern at a PR agency in New York. He takes his roommate along with him when he goes out to a bar or dance club. "I go out with Jeff and have him watch as I walk past the bar or through a crowded area of guys to see who watches me and who is checking me out. Then I do the same for him. If we see that some guys are just watching everything that walks by, then he's not a candidate anymore, but if a cutie is checking me out, I'll figure out a way to bump into him near the bar and say hi."

Group Play

You see a guy you're interested in. You've made the "I'm interested" eye contact. But he's with a group of guys. How do you approach him? Men behave differently in groups than they do one-on-one. When a straight man walks up to a group of women, the motive is obvious—he's interested in one of them. When a man walks up to a group of other men—especially gay men—the group instantly clicks into competitive mode. We size up the new guy and, if he's interesting, we start attempting to outdo one another for his attention.

Walking up to a group of guys can be very intimidating. You never know if they're all just friends, or if some are couples, or if they're all coworkers, or if they're just huddling together for warmth like Eskimos. If you want to cast a wide net, go ahead and flirt with the whole lot of 'em. This is where our male competitive nature can work to your advantage. When a flirt is on the line, you can play guys off one another for your attention.

To do this successfully, you have to flirt with all of the guys in the group—even the ones you aren't attracted to. Talking with the whole group will give you a chance to introduce yourself in a nonthreatening way (no one man feels like he's on the spot). And by flirting with the whole bunch you show that you're not just being opportunistic—you're not just blindly casting into the wind to see who takes your bait (even if you actually are). Talk with the guys, but pay careful attention to see who is sending out positive body-language signals.

If you don't want to approach a group, your best bet may be to wait until the guy you have your eye on leaves the group momentarily. Now's your chance to find a reason to talk to him. The direct approach usually works well. Just go up and say, "Hi, my name is [insert name here] and I wanted to introduce myself but didn't want to interrupt you and your friends."

Don't Sit With Your Crew All Night

You know how hard it is to go up to a guy and say hi when he's with a group of friends. Now suppose a cutie wants to roll up on you, but you're surrounded by the guys who came to the bar with you, none of whom are going to take you home. Do the other guys a favor by giving yourself plenty of alone-time: time when you leave your pals to take a stroll around the party, just to see where the cute guys are, and to let them know that you don't have a boyfriend in tow.

Kevin, 26, an aspiring muralist from Brooklyn, explains

how easy it is: "Your buddies will understand if you tell them that hanging out with them all night is going to cramp your style. They don't want to be cock-blockers, so they'll understand if you slip off to check out the action in other parts of the place."

Complicated Compliments

Every guy likes to be complimented. Flattery can get you places that a platinum card cannot, but woe is the man who delivers a ham-fisted line when a unique compliment is required.

"You're very handsome" is something plenty of men would love to hear, but it's specific to neither the complimentor nor complimentee. A handsome guy who's heard that one before will not necessarily feel that your compliment is genuine. It will sound like a line. Make your flattery specific and heartfelt, and do it sparingly. To impress a guy, give him a unique compliment that other people might not have given him before. Try these bits of aural honey on for size, and don't forget to throw in a bit of humor:

"I've always been a big fan of Lynda Carter. Where did you get that great Wonder Woman T-shirt? May I try it on?"

"Wow, I never see guys ordering a gin martini anymore. My uncle used to do that too. But I bet you're a much better kisser."

"I'll bet your boyfriend will be angry when he sees us kissing in a minute. Oh, you don't have a boyfriend?"

Nice is a Four-letter Word

Nice is one of those adjectives that's fine for drapes and the weather, but it's a foul word when it comes to hooking up.

Give guys good compliments. Make them smile with your sly humor. But whatever you do, don't be too nice. If you approach a guy and act too nice, he'll immediately put you into the sexless potential-friend category. You'll have a pleasant conversation, and then he'll move on to other guys—guys who aren't so nice but who are going to really put his bedsprings to the test. Nice gets no play.

If you're meeting a man for the first time, don't flatter him too much. If you're talking up a new acquaintance over the phone trying to make a date, don't call too often—and make sure you hang up first, at the peak of the phone call when you're both having the most fun. Don't speak with a tentative voice. Be authoritative, not nice.

Don't be overly accommodating. This technique works really well for Lucky, 25, a fitness instructor in Los Angeles. "Say you bump into a guy in a museum when you were both looking at the Aztec calendars and he asks you to wait there while he goes to the bathroom. This is assuming, of course, that he doesn't want you to follow him to the bathroom yet. If you can tell he's up for that, then tell him you'll join him. But if he asks you to wait there in the pre-Colombian exhibit, don't agree to it. Tell him instead that you'll meet him at the museum café instead, or in the Oceania exhibit in the next room. You won't do his bidding, and he'll think it's exciting. Tiny little gestures like that will create a more forceful impression of you in his mind, and he'll be drawn to you. It works like a charm."

Rather than bashfully accept a compliment, make your remark a confident one. When he says, "I really like your shoes. Where'd you get them?" respond with a swaggering, "I'm not telling you because then all the hot guys will be falling all over you!" A bit of overconfidence—without being rude—is ideal. You're not aiming for Miss Congeniality here, so don't be worried that you'll hurt his feelings.

While you're at it, banish the word *fun* from your vocabulary. Don't use it in an e-mail. It might seem fine to write, "I had fun talking with you. Want to grab a cup of coffee?" but it's something you might write to a coworker or friend, and it won't get you laid. Try something more forceful. A more effective approach would be to write, "When can I take you out for a drink? I want to finish our conversation."

Lucky sums it up well. "If you're throwing yourself at his feet, he'll assume that he can get the same treatment from anyone, and he'll be less likely to stick around with you."

Third Time's the Charm

One look won't tell him you're interested. One groin bump up against him as you walk through a crowd won't either. The second time could just be a coincidence. It takes repeated physical contact, or a repeated nonverbal cue—usually the third time's the charm—to convey to him that you are interested. If you do catch his eye a third time, you can be sure he knows that you mean business. Now you've got to go up and say hi.

Be Direct

Once you've charmed and giggled with and wooed the guy until he's putty in your hands, that's the time you've got to pounce—go in for the thrill. You've done everything right. You've acted confident—maybe a little bit cocky. You've given him good body language. And you're reading his signals too, and they're telling you to come up and see him sometime.

Be direct. Ask him, "Do you want to go home with me?"

If you need a situation, create one. If you've reached a

bar's closing hour before you've sealed the deal, this is a perfect chance to invite him home with you. Just don't linger too long trying to get him to initiate a rendezvous. There's an expiration date on every hot flirtation. It varies from flirt to flirt, but all flirts must come to an end.

With luck and a little work, your flirtation will end with his clothes in a pile at the foot of your bed. If the flirt doesn't move in that direction before the moment passes, your tête-à-tête runs the risk of petering out and dying without any bump-'n'-grind. If you've been chatting with him for a while and things are going well, but the conversation keeps going on, you're in danger of becoming a friend candidate, and that's the end of your chances of bedding him. Before you lose the chance to play doctor, ask him, "What are you doing now? I'd like you to come home with me." The direct approach always gets a direct answer.

Smile Like You Mean it

Smile while you're looking him over; smile when you're touching his arm. Smiling when you're dealing with him won't always put him at ease, but that's not what you're after anyway. You want there to be some sexual tension in your interaction.

Smiling does several things for you. First, it makes him wonder what you're thinking. That little bit of mystery works to your advantage. Second, it lets him know that you're enjoying yourself because you're with him. Third, it conveys the idea that you're positive, comfortable, and up for a good time. You'll catch more flies with honey—so give 'em some honey and make sure you smile as you talk to him.

Karma's a Bitch

How you react to guys who come up to flirt with you will

affect your standing as well. If someone you aren't attracted to comes up and gives you the elevator eyes and pays you a smart, funny, cocky compliment, you *must* be polite. Gay men notice pick-up action going on around them. If you roll your eyes or laugh him off, karma will bite you in the ass. Other guys will see how shabbily you treated him, and only the most cynical, hateful homos will talk to you after that.

Guys get drunk in bars, so a frisky fella might feel you up without so much as a by-your-leave. Do not react with haste and indignity. You can be a gentleman, albeit a confident one. Don't say or do anything that would embarrass the guy as you lift his drunk ass off the floor and scoot him along his merry way. Do act like you'd want to be treated if one of your flirtations got out of hand in the most messy, inebriated way possible.

If someone sober walks up and says hi, shake his hand, introduce yourself, and give him the courtesy of a moment or two of your time—after all, you know how hard it is to approach people. Then, if he hasn't become more interesting in the intervening moments, say, "It was very nice to meet you, Gary," and excuse yourself to find a friend, use the bathroom, go to the dance floor, etc.

Even if it's just for a one-night stand, you don't want to attract the assholes who think it's funny when you mistreat someone. As gay men, we already have to deal with enough shit—please, let's not shovel more of it on each other. Let's try to treat each other well.

Stay Positive

Nothing drags a conversation down faster than negativity. Though you may have had a rough day at the office, and your houseplants have all died, and your cat just used your damask chaise as a scratching post, *the hot guy with his hand on your ass doesn't care.*

Avoid negative talk at all costs. Being wooed by a downer is tedious, irritating, and—above all—unsexy. Be positive in what you say about yourself as well. You won't be projecting confidence if you're mired in reporting that you're no good at this or you suck at that.

While you're staying positive, remember to never ever bring up your ex. (Or your exes—especially if several are in the room.) The guy you're hitting on may be next for you, but he won't want to hear"Next!" in his head. No one wants to feel like a deli counter ticket.

Let Him Know You've Noticed Him

This tactic works best someplace other than a bar or club environment. The technique involves conveying to a guy that you've noticed him before, but without saying so directly.

Martin, 24, a graduate student in Austin, has had this technique used on him before, and it worked so well, he's used it ever since on other guys. "I was at the video store dropping off some tapes a friend had rented. I'd never even been to the place before, which is why this approach surprised me so much. The store was almost entirely empty except for the clerk, and it was almost closing time. I'd never seen him before, but as I was turning to go, he said, 'I like your new haircut.' I *had* just gotten one, but not knowing the guy, I was so surprised that he said it that I did a double take. I looked at his name badge to see if I recognized the name, and I didn't. I asked him if we'd met and he just said, 'No, but I've noticed you before.' It was sweet. We started talking and he asked me to go to coffee with him as soon as he locked up. I agreed, but we never made it to coffee—instead we fucked in the backroom of the video store. His line still would have worked if I hadn't just gotten a haircut though."

And as for using the technique on other guys? "Well, it works well for guys I've met and guys I haven't," says Martin, "but it works best in places like the library at school or the grocery store—places where it's possible I might have seen someone before."

Listen

You can gather information that will be useful to you in your seduction techniques simply by listening. While you're watching for body language cues from guys you're interested in, make sure you tune in your ears too. What they talk about will give you great data about what's occupying his mind, what his likes or dislikes are, and ways into a conversation with him.

If you go up to a cute guy and say, "Hi. How are you?" he may give you some clues as to how to pursue the conversation. "Glad I finally got a drink! That line at the bar was so long." You've got your in. Talk about how crowded the place is, or offer to buy his next drink.

Focus on what he's saying rather than on a need to fill the silences with chatter. Simple questions can prompt answers that will spark conversations. For a few conversation starters, try:

- "Have you ever heard this DJ spin before?"
- "Have you ever been to this gallery/club/prison before?"
- "Have you ever used this detergent before?"

Take it Step-by-step

You certainly don't have to incorporate all these techniques into your game the next time you go out. Take it slow and try one new technique at a time until you feel comfortable with the way it should work and you're getting a result. The best way to make any skill here work well is if you incorporate it into your own personal style—you don't want to be too uncomfortable. It's the personality equivalent of wearing someone else's clothes. By integrating these methods into your cruising techniques one at a time, you won't overload, but you'll gradually become more attractive to the guys who interest you.

Then just relax and take a step back from your cruising. Trust that you've made an impression. If he likes what he sees, he'll soon be coming after you.

To successfully get laid, you have to know where to find men. So let's talk location. Simply put, gay men are anywhere *you* are and then some. Look behind you. We're everywhere.

We often tend to congregate in safe clumps, like in big cities, gay bars, and musical theater productions, where we know we can find one other, not get harassed, and hook up for a little man-on-man action. For the uninitiated, the spots listed below are good places to start your manhunt. Gay bars are the likeliest of hook-up spots, but there are a dozen other good locales to visit in the search for sex, whether you're in a big town or a small one. In large cities, you'll find a variety of types of gay bars and clubs, and other big-city amenities like giant dance clubs, bathhouses, sex clubs, and organized events like jack-off parties. But even in smaller burgs with smaller gay populations, you may find a queer watering hole, a cruisy park, or a mall bathroom that can provide ample action. Knowing how to find these places and what you'll encounter when you get there will help make your cruising more efficient and effective.

The trick to tracking down a hot trick is to know what types of guys tend to be found in what types of locations. With the help of a few expert cruising friends, I've prepared a list of an assortment of gay places, what to expect in different environments, the kinds of men likely to be found there, and pitfalls to avoid when you're cruising in these locations.

We'll explore both conventional places and unconventional ones, including:

- Bars
- Clubs
- Bathhouses
- Gay resorts
- Cruisy parks
- Local gay magazines
- Jack-off parties
- Gourmet food markets
- Gay sports clubs
- Gay film festivals
- Art museums and galleries
- Galas and benefits
- Theaters
- Hardware stores

Gay Bars

As I mentioned above, the gay bar is the quintessential homosexual gathering place. Like a desert oasis or a savanna pool left after the rainy season, gay bars collect all species of homosexual, who come to drink, commune, and mate—at least for the night. Before we could be out of the closet publicly, bars were furtive gathering places where we could meet, talk, entertain one another, and—certainly—hook up. Not only were gay bars central to early gay community culture, a gay bar was the site of the launch of the modern gay liberation movement, which began with the 1969 Stonewall riots at New York City's Stonewall Inn. Bars, for better or worse, have remained a central part of gay culture ever since.

In large cities you'll find dozens of bars, each with a different vibe and each with a different clientele ranging from young to old and from trendy to blissfully trend-free. There are bars that cater to special interests, like leather, Levi's, hookers, go-go dancing, or drag. There are hands-off places where the point is primarily to be seen, and there are bars where you're more likely to be felt up than looked in the eye. Because bars vary so widely in patronage and sexual temperature, it will do you good to know the difference between the many types of gay bars. (Note: Not all bars are gay every night of the week—do your homework and call ahead if you've never been before to find out what nights are gay or gay-popular.)

Neighborhood Bars

"This kind of place used to be a joke to me," says Gary, 29, a sound engineer in Chicago. "I used to think they were only places for old guys and barflies. But now they're my favorite kind of place. They're good for hooking up around happy-hour time, especially if you get to know the bartender. The place in my neighborhood has this sexy Pakistani guy behind the bar, and if I stop in after work, he'll tell me if there are any cuties in the place, especially if they're there alone. Plus they have a beer bust every Sunday night, and cheap beer is always good for getting new guys to talk and flirt. If I want to buy a guy a few beers to get him loosened up, it only sets me back a couple of bucks." Ah, the economy shtup.

At a neighborhood bar (NB), the beer is usually a bargain

and the music in the jukebox is often quite old—and not always in a cool, ironic way. NBs are also great for young guys who enjoy the attention of older guys. The danger of an NB is that it's the kind of place that attracts regulars. *Don't sleep with the regulars.* They're called regulars because they come back regularly. Cross a regular by not calling him back or tossing him out after tossing him off, and you might develop a bad, mojo-crushing reputation around the bar. Also, tip the bartender well, but don't sleep with him. If you're bad in bed (perhaps he fed you too many drinks and your soldier refused to go into battle) or if you ditch him unceremoniously, everyone at the bar will hear about it. NBs can be gossipy places.

Who you can meet: Depending on the neighborhood, you'll meet barflies, older guys, 'hood rats, guys who like to read in bars, an assortment of low-maintenance cuties (especially if the bar has a good party/club/stripper/beer-bust night), and friends of the bartender.

What to watch out for: Regulars (don't fuck them), barflies, and bartenders (don't fuck them!)

Potential come-ons: "Buy you a beer?"

Hustler Bars

These bars, naturally, are good for picking up a date. And they're places where you don't have to know any of the seduction techniques you are learning in this book.

You might never know if the bar you're planning to go to is of the hustler bar (HB) variety. For legal reasons, it's a bad idea to advertise your establishment as a hangout for sex workers. So word of mouth is usually the only way to know you're venturing into hustler territory.

HBs can be jovial places or they can be totally grim. Keith, 44, who frequents a well-known HB near his apartment in Boston, says, "Guys who are looking to hire are very often totally open about the fact, and they go into the place looking for a good time. It can be a lot of fun because it's unlikely you'll be turned down for sex if the price is right. We know why other guys are there—to hook up too—and we joke and laugh about it. A bar I used to go to on business trips in Las Vegas was another matter. In that place, lots of closeted and married guys would go looking to hire a hot young thing for an hour or two. But they were freaked out about being recognized or feeling guilty. Some of them were all business and no play, and the atmosphere was pretty severe. Other bars there were more relaxed."

If you're young and pretty and not looking to be hired for your talents, then you might consider moving on down the road to the next bar. The hookers won't take kindly to your cramping their style. And the customers will be upset if they offer you the going rate and you turn them down.

Who you can meet: Hustlers, johns

What to watch out for: Hustlers, johns

Potential come-ons: "Spend some time with me?"

Trendy Bars

This kind of bar is often a building rehabilitated from an old paper factory or insane asylum, or it's a previously hot trendy bar (TB) that has become the new hot TB—the spot to hang out in the most fleeting of fashions draped over bodies with extraordinarily low body-fat percentages. Midsize cities can really only sustain one or two TBs at a time, whereas larger cites tend to have several. They pop up here and there, usurping one another's claims as the new "it" place in a gay ghetto.

Abdulkareem, 31, a personal shopper and stylist in Los Angeles, likes these bars but knows they're not the greatest pick-up spots. He says, "I like the goofy flourishes they put in there to make the bridge and tunnel crowd go 'Ooh!' like unisex bathrooms and foot pedals for the sinks rather than knobs, and little lights embedded in the bar. But mostly I go there because I love to watch the pretty people." Of one TB in West Hollywood, Abdulkareem says, "It's always full of actors and wannabes. I've seen more than one closeted actor waltz in with a 'girlfriend.' Guys here are far more interested in looking to see who else just walked in than they are in hooking up. I've seen the joyless pretty people hook up, but can you imagine how boring that sex was?

"The attitude can be a bit much. Guys in this kind of place are always looking to fuck up the ladder. There's plenty of irony and sarcasm flying around the room. These are my people, but if I want action I go someplace else. If I like a guy I see in that place, I have to be really bold to get his attention. Or I lie and say I'm a casting agent. I just have to make sure he's not there with a fruit-fly girlfriend. The girlfriends of pretty boys can make it impossible to hook up. They get jealous."

Who you can meet: Guys with big pecs, guys wearing designer clothes, and other pretty people

What to watch out for: Bitter, sarcastic queens, and their cockblocking "girlfriends"

Potential come-ons: "Love that shirt. Can I touch you?"

Leather and Levi's Bars

The leather and Levi's (L&L) bars draw a very specific crowd. The typical customer is over 30, prefers jeans and plain white T-shirts to couture, is often fond of leather (a fetish that often—though not always—intersects with **BDSM** play), and likes other guys who are into the same stuff.

The L&L bar is a prominent part of most gay communities in the Unites States. Aided by the spreading of the bear movement worldwide, L&L bars can be found most everywhere now. Boyd, our 35-year-old computer guy in Tulsa, prefers this kind of bar. "I'm not really a bear myself," he says, "and I've never been in a sling, but there is something about the guys in this place that really turns me on. There's lots of facial hair, lots of grabbing going on, and these guys just seem totally sexually liberated. I graduated to this type of bar after spending lots of time in the trendy and twinkie bars. These places are a lot easier to get laid in too. The guys just seem much more relaxed about hooking up.

"I've got the perfect line for this place. I lean close to a guy I'm talking to and say, 'Phew! I've got some serious BO going on. Sorry about that...unless you like that.' They always like that."

Who you can meet: Otters and bears and cubs, oh my!

What to watch out for: Stubble-burn on your face—or, if you're lucky, on your ass cheeks

Potential come-ons: Don't shower. They'll come to you.

Dance Clubs

These places vary in size and scope too, and the crowd can change from night to night. The clientele is largely determined by the DJ and the music he or she is spinning. Kevin, the muralist in Brooklyn, loves to visit big dance clubs when he is traveling. "You really have to get a sense of the music that's going to be played at a club if you're interested in going," he says. "It's not because one crowd is better than the other, but the music can draw in different crowds in clubs. Most clubs draw in guys in their 20s and 30s.

"The top-40 crowd likes to dance and drink and mess around. The guys that go to hear those DJs want to hear songs they know, and unless it's an 18-and-up club, they're not hung up on looking like rock stars. The under-21s need to loosen up a bit! The '80s and '90s crowd is pretty easygoing, but those guys are in their 30s. The music sucks if you ask me, but the men are willing to get it on, especially if you dance up next to them. You've got to stay away from anyone who gets up on a box to dance for the crowd. It can be tragic.

"A jungle or deep-house night will bring in young guys who are more interested in the music and the groove than hooking up. The best way to start talking with a guy is to wait until he goes outside for a break or to light a cigarette, and talk to him about the music, about the DJ, if he dropped the beat, or if he mixed well, or other DJs you like. You gotta brush up on your DJ knowledge if you're gonna try this, though. Talking up a Frankie Knuckles fan on Digweed is going to be a mess.

"There are big circuit party-type DJs at big arenas in lots of cities, but the best places are clubs that have rooms with different kinds of music. There's a place in LA with a hip-hop room upstairs, a Latin room, and a house main room. It's got a great mix of hot Latin, black, and white guys. It's totally hot to see cholos and b-boys making out with each other, and the sexual energy goes higher the sweatier it gets. I do pretty well in those places once I weed out the tweakers. It helps that I have some killer moves."

Who you can meet: Guys who like to dance (and they're often sweaty and inebriated)

What to watch out for: Tweakers and drunk show-offs who like to dance on the platforms

Potential come-ons: Getting real close to talk to a cutie because the music is loud

Sex Clubs

Moving away from bars and dance clubs, we get to the sex-focused venues. (Often these are places guys go to after a night out at the bars and clubs.) There are two main varieties of sex-focused establishments: sex clubs and bathhouses. At sex clubs, one generally pays an entrance fee to get in, and guys remain dressed or partially dressed (in underwear or jockstraps) while they cruise mazes, common areas, and dark corners set up with glory holes. Sex takes place out in the open, and threesomes—or more-somes—are common. Sex clubs, more so than bathhouses, attract a specific kind of man or cater to a certain fetish. Some sex clubs are leather-inspired. Some have clientele who skew younger or older. Some cater to specific ethnic groups.

"It's virtually guaranteed action," says Timothy, 35, a social worker in Philadelphia. "The places aren't tea lounges. They smell like sweat and sex. The sex is kind of dirty and totally anonymous usually. The places I've been are busy on Sundays and late nights on weekends, after guys have been out cruising bars. Lots of them were unlucky at the bars, so they go where they have a good chance of sucking dick or fucking."

Who you can meet: Guys who aren't that interested in chitchat

What to watch out for: Speed, poppers, and messy guys who are interested in unsafe sex because their judgement is impaired

Potential come-ons: Just reach out and touch someone.

Bathhouses

Bathhouses differ from sex clubs in that men pay the entrance fee, are given a towel and a condom, and get a locker or a private room to put their clothes in. They shower (hopefully), wrap the towels around their waists, and wander the hallways, showers, pools, steam rooms, dry saunas, Jacuzzis, or mazes that are set up for cruising. Sex is usually prohibited in the common areas, so most of the action takes place behind closed doors or in the steam rooms. Many establishments specifically prohibit sex in their rules, despite having given you a condom. By the way, there are "straight" bathhouses (often Turkish or Russian-run) where sex is definitely not on the menu. Make sure the place you're headed is gay.

Trey, the PR intern in New York, visits bathhouses occasionally. "I like that guys go there with an agenda," he says. "I think that's really hot. You have to be up front with guys, though. If you're not interested in someone who approaches you, you have to say no right away, without being rude."

My first book, *101 Gay Sex Secrets Revealed,* goes into bathhouse etiquette in more detail. Suffice to say here that even though it's a place specifically geared toward having sex, you have to be a little forward to get action at a bathhouse. Go up and say hi, or convey your interest by gently putting your hand on the thigh of the guy next to you in the steam room. If he turns you down, honor that. This is not a place to convince a guy of your charms. Shower between encounters. If you're HIV-positive, tell your partners before you engage in any behavior that would put them at risk. Always use condoms. Men don't discuss HIV status at bathhouses as often as they should.

Who you can meet: Naked guys in towels

What to watch out for: Guys who won't take a gentle "no" for an answer

Potential come-ons: A tip of the head or a gesture to follow you is often all it takes

Gay Resorts

Seth, 42, a salesman from Orlando, loves to take his vacations at gay resorts in Fort Lauderdale, Provincetown, Palm Springs, the Russian River Valley, and Key West. He often stays at clothing-optional resorts, but sometimes prefers plain old gay B&Bs.

"The guys that go to these vacation places are rarely under 30, but that's fine by me. I prefer guys my age and older anyway. But occasionally there will be a cute young guy or two. They travel in pairs, it seems. Eye candy is always nice, even if that's not who I like to go to bed with.

"Even at the clothing-optional resorts, conversation is absolutely required. It's not like these are bathhouses, even if they're advertised that way. If I see a hot guy reading a book or sunning himself, I go up and introduce myself. Lots of these places have a poolside happy hour too. And since everyone here is on vacation from somewhere, it's easy to ask where he's from and if he's been here before. By that point, I can sense whether he's interested in talking more. If he is, I'll get closer and put my hand on his thigh and ask if he'd like to go to my room for a drink.

"It's great because there's no pretense of a long-term relationship. Everyone has to drive or fly back home, so it's just hot vacation sex. Guys are always horny, and tourists and vacationing guys are even hornier because there is this expectation of having a hot memory when you get home from vacation."

Who you can meet: Horny vacationing men

What to watch out for: Falling for a guy who lives a thousand miles away

Potential come-ons: "Where are you from? Never heard of it. Show me on the atlas in my room."

Cruisy Parks

Cruising for sex in public parks is illegal everywhere in the United States. There are no legally sanctioned outdoor wilderness fuck spots, so if you're interested in cruising the great outdoors, you have to be aware that you're doing something illegal. Don't sue me if you get busted in the talking forests with a cock in your mouth.

You have been warned.

Parks and wilderness areas have long been cruising spots for guys who are looking for a little anonymous, open-air sex. Lukas, 33, a Web designer in Simi Valley, California, has long enjoyed cruising parks. "There was a great city park where I used to live, and it was warm year-round so there was an abundance of guys hooking up all the time. This park had hills and tree coverage and hiking trails, and guys would just hang out by the heads of these little trails that led off into the woods, trying to look casual like they're just enjoying the scenery.

"All you have to do is go up and say hi, or make eye contact and grab your dick through your pants. Then just follow him off to the wooded out-of-sight area and drop your pants. There was a great place for nude sunbathing too. You can pretty much guess that anywhere there are naked guys, guys are fucking in the bushes. You do have to watch out for police, though. Thank God I never got arrested, but I know people who have been, and it can really fuck up your life for a long time."

There are Web sites that provide listings of places you might visit if you're cruising for sex, including the best times of day to find action and whether there have been arrests there recently. Even though, generally speaking, police officers who cruise the spots undercover are not allowed to whip out their dicks to entrap you, some will do just that anyway, then deny that it happened. It's a common misconception that a police officer must tell you he's a cop if you ask him. He is not obligated to tell you anything.

Some guys wait to be approached by a quickie trick, assuming it's safer and that therefore your playmate isn't a cop. Trust your instincts. If the guy cruising you looks or acts fishy, don't risk a quickie. It's horribly unfair that gay men are prosecuted far more rigorously for public sex than straight people are, but the best thing you can do until attitudes change is to protect yourself from entrapment.

Who you can meet: Guys fond of fast and furious action al fresco

What to watch out for: Undercover cops

Potential come-ons: "Hi."

Local Gay Magazines

In your local gay magazine or newspaper you'll often find a section with personal and classified ads with escorts, massage therapists, naked carpenters, naked computer repairmen, naked house cleaners, etc. The popularity of print personals has been steadily declining in the gay community since the advent of the online hookup profile, but it's still the preferred method for guys who aren't in a hurry to get laid (or who have a legitimate need for a naked guy with a feather duster). It takes a while to mail a letter or call the mailbox of a guy whose description you like, so consider your calendar when wooing a regular joe (as opposed to an escort).

"I'm all for meeting hot guys," says Buck, 37, an emergency room nurse from Nashville. "But guys who use the newspaper are often guys who don't have a computer. Their photos can be older than online pictures would be. Plus, since anyone can just pick up the rag with your photo in it, there are lots of headless pictures of guys who don't want to be recognized for their 'zest for life' ads. If you want a haircut from a naked guy, you can't beat the local rags."

Who you can meet: Technophobes, escorts, naked barbers, headless torsos

What to watch out for: Guys who were hot in 1987—and who are still using a photo from that year in their classified ad

Potential come-ons: "I'm writing to you because I saw your ad, and I too enjoy long walks on the beach, sunsets, and rainy days."

Jack-off Parties

Jack-off parties are popular in larger cities. This specialized form of sex party exhibits wildly varying membership requirements and allowable activities, all at the discretion of the host. Participation in some groups is restricted to guys of a certain age or physique (which usually means no overweight guys). Other hosts welcome all body types and all ages.

"I've been to parties where you check your clothes and you're encouraged to jerk off other guys or suck them off too," says Martin, the graduate student. "Other parties don't allow you to touch other guys at all. The ones where you have to pay to get in usually have stricter rules about touching."

Ah, slutty youth. They say it's wasted on the slutty young, but Martin, for one, is an equal-opportunity jerker: "The parties with all young guys are fun, but the energy can be more exciting at the all-welcome parties, even if there are fewer six-pack abs. Hell, a nice, hard dick is great no matter who it's attached to."

On the spectrum of activities that are more or less likely to transmit HIV/AIDS or other STDs, solo masturbation in the company of others is a very safe way to play. It's not as safe if mutual masturbation, oral or anal sex, or exposure to others' ejaculate is involved. Stroking your dick using another guy's come as lube isn't risk-free, as there is some chance of access to your urethral opening, which is lined with mucous membranes.

Your best bet for finding jack-off clubs is an online search for "jack-off party" or "the jacks," as they're sometimes known.

Who you can meet: Voyeurs and exhibitionists

What to watch out for: Guys who won't follow the house rules

Potential come-ons: "Help a buddy out?"

Gourmet Food Markets

Santiago is a manager at a Los Angeles gourmet food market. These are places that offer organic foods, a wide selection from local wineries, and more cheese than an episode of *American Idol.* In Los Angeles, as in other cities, they're a big hit with the homos. "I see guys in this place all the time scoring," says Santiago. "Guys ask me for help all the time with picking out a bottle of wine or asking which fresh pasta is best, stuff like that. I get hit on here too, and I've even pulled a couple of guys into the loading-dock area and I've gotten blown a few times there. One guy brought a bottle of honey with him and licked honey off my dick. Of course it was organic honey.

"The only guys I steer clear of are the ones trying to impress me with their elaborate gourmet dishes. If they're buying a pound of truffles and want to cook me fabulous dinners, I can tell right away they're (a) high maintenance, and (b) looking for a boyfriend. I'm happy being single now."

Who you can meet: Gay gourmands. Even guys who are vegetarians at home like a little hot meat every now and then.

What to watch out for: Guys looking to cook you dinner—for the rest of your life

Potential come-ons: "I'm looking for the freshest meat here. Can you help me?"

Gay Sports Clubs

Gay softball, soccer, swim, rugby, and other sports clubs or teams can be found in many parts of the country. Athletic-minded guys getting sweaty on the playing field get to check out each other's toned, sweaty bodies.

Marcos, 31, was on a gay soccer team in Los Angeles for three years and got plenty of play, often from members of the opposing teams. "When you're playing against another gay

team, you have to talk tough and be competitive, but half the guys on my team were total queens—which I loved. It wasn't smart to hook up with them though, because if you're good as a team, you travel with them to tournaments and competitions out of town, and you don't want to get too jealous and *Real World* on each other. You become more like brothers.

"But sometimes you'll meet a hot guy on an opposing team," he continues. "We go out for drinks after the games a lot of times, and you get a chance to meet other teams. You get to knock each other around on the field, then you can take them home after a game, especially if they're from out of town. You can even wear your uniforms if you're into that."

Who you can meet: Competitive, athletic guys in uniforms—with jockstraps

What to watch out for: Overly competitive guys, fellow teammates

Potential come-ons: "Call that a goal? I'll show you how to score," and "If I make a goal, you have to give me your phone number."

Gay Film Festivals

Gay film festivals typically bring out an over-30 crowd, unless you count the volunteers and staff, who are often novice filmmakers or other would-be film industry hopefuls. Lou, 41, a roving film festival programmer originally from Philadelphia, has had flings with both film buffs and a few volunteers.

"I've worked for film festivals for, like, 15 years," he reports, "and gay festivals are the best. Everyone is determined to have a good time, and they don't care how bad the films are. Sometimes they are awful, and I should know: I've selected a few.

"Because people often travel into town for the bigger events, it's good to know of a place nearby you can sneak off to if you score some booty. When I'm in San Francisco, there's a storage room that's never locked in one of the theaters. It's musty, but my playmate of the hour usually doesn't care.

"When I'm at one of my festivals in October, the hotel I usually stay at is right around the corner from one of the theaters. You can spot the VIP ticket holders right away, because of the color of their badges. I usually steer clear of them if I'm working for the festival. The staff and volunteers usually wear a different color badge. Volunteers I'll bag, but not staff. For working guys, we usually have to wait until after hours or until after a screening has started, because otherwise one of us has to run off to do something. At the midnight screenings, I love to sit in back and see who gets up to use the bathroom. If he's hot, then I duck out just behind him and follow him to the bathroom, just to see if I can catch his eye. I definitely get some play that way."

Who you can meet: Men of all ages who are into cinema (or who are at least into the gay sex scenes)

What to watch out for: Lesbian movies, filmfest pseudo-intellectuals ("I feel that Araki's *Splendor* marked the end of New Queer Cinema, don't you?"), and actors

Potential come-ons: "Do you prefer François Ozon's sex scenes or Sebastien Lifshitz's?"

Art Museums and Galleries

Two kinds of people go to art museums and galleries. The first kind are men who truly appreciate art, and the second kind are men who feel that they must go to art museums and galleries, despite their ambivalence about art, because they think artiness is expected of them.

Carter, 25, is a docent on the weekends at a Chicago museum. "I lead these tours around the galleries on

Saturdays, and sometimes there are guys who watch me throughout the tour—not the paintings. People get close to each other without noticing it when they're really into looking intently at the pieces, but I can tell when guys are getting close to me just to get close. It's hot. I've invited guys to the café afterward for coffee, and I've gone home with a few too."

"I love going to the antiquities exhibits and watching the guys who check out the Greek statuary," says T.J., 30, a free-lance writer in Los Angeles. "There's something very erotic about those sculptures with the huge muscles and the perfect

wavy hair. If I can tell guys are bored because they're there feeling like they ought to go just because they're in town, then I get close and ask if they've seen the Egyptian exhibit. If they start talking, I get a sense of whether they're there with someone, and whether he's gay—though I can usually tell that by the parts of the exhibit he's looking at."

Who you can meet: Men of all ages

What to watch out for: Artists and European tourists who may only *look* gay.

Potential come-ons: "Have you seen the Flemish life-drawings? They're very realistic."

Gay Galas

Ben, 26, prefers big-ticket fund-raisers and gala parties. Because he works in development at a GLBT nonprofit organization in Los Angeles, he often gets free tickets to fund-raiser events from donors. "The tickets to these gala parties sometimes cost more than $300 per person, but often the donors I know buy the tickets to make the contribution, then they can't attend. So I'm often the youngest person in the room by a dozen years. It's perfect, because I prefer older guys. The trick to hooking up at these things is to find the guys who don't want a boyfriend. Not all of them want to be sugar daddies, but some do.

"I just squeeze up next to a hot daddy—my type—at the host bar and when he turns around, I ask him to order me a cocktail, whatever he's having. Then I make sure I tip the bartenders for both of us. That's usually all it takes to get him talking to me. I don't ask his name if he doesn't offer it, but I always touch his thigh or bicep, and I look right at him while I'm taking a sip.

"The last time was with a buff guy wearing a great Marc Jacobs tie: I asked if he'd show me where the coat check is, and he offered to show me. When I was behind him, I got close again and grabbed his ass. He grabbed my hand and pulled me toward the stairs. We went to an upstairs storage room at the top floor of this place above the silent auction tables and we sucked each other off, then he said he had to go back downstairs but he invited me back to his place after the event. I waited a few minutes before going down the other stairs, then I saw him going up on stage to give a speech. He was one of the event bigwigs!"

Who you can meet: Thirty-, 40-, and 50-somethings with a social conscience and a full wallet

What to watch out for: I truly love our lesbian sisters (they've done plenty for you and me), but some dykes at nonprofit GLBT organizations will harangue you for hooking up at a "serious event."

Potential come-ons: "Do you mind showing me to the coat check?" Works even if you're not wearing a coat, and it's summer.

Theaters

"You'd be surprised at the number of men I've picked up in movie theaters," says Oliver, 36, a friend who works in film production in Los Angeles. "Not porn theaters, mind you—first-run, honest-to-goodness movie theaters. I retitled *Looking for Richard* 'Looking for Dick.' The guy who I chatted with in line before the film then sat next to me during the film. Afterward we drove to Griffith Park, and he became my one American outdoor encounter. But my crowning glory was a [mall] screening of the kids' movie *Fly Away Home.* I was there with my friend and her grandmother; the other guy was there with his aunt—a nun. It was a small theater, so naturally I had to sit next to the attractive man. After a movie's worth of fondling and exploration, we both just had to run into the bathroom at the movie's end and finish what we had started.

"As far as advice for future moviegoers, I'd say the key is sitting near to your prey before the movie begins. If you're both there alone, make up some lame excuse about hating to sit alone and ask if you can join him. Trust me—it's actually worked. And then, just let your fingers do the walking. I've had some failures. One guy in Prague got up and moved: Apparently, I'd misread the signal. I've had some wild successes too, including with a film producer at the Broadway revival of *Nine*. In any case, there's nothing more thrilling to me than being part of an captive audience."

Who you can meet: Practically everyone goes to the movies. At matinees (where crowds are thinnest), you'll find students, the unemployed, and guys with night jobs.

What to watch out for: Ushers, soccer moms (at kids' movies), homophobes (at action movies)

Potential come-ons: Drop some popcorn in his lap and reach for it. ("Oops! Oh, sorry...Or am I?")

Hardware Stores

File this one under nontraditional pick-up spots. It's a favorite of my friend Lucky. Lucky, 25, is a fitness instructor in Los Angeles, where a few of the larger home improvement stores stay open 24 hours. "Men go in there at 2 A.M. looking for...a circular saw?" he says. "Yeah, right. If you're looking for a butch guy, head for the hardware. If you like more effeminate guys, look in the home decor department by the paint chips. All kinds of guys hang out by the plants.

"The hookup can be pretty easy. If I'm interested in a guy in the paint department, I'll hold up two paint chips and ask if he prefers 'butter-cream' or 'sugar-cookie' yellow. If he responds at all, it's not hard for me to insert into the conversation that it's my bedroom that I need to have painted. He invariably tells me—if he's looking to hook up—that he'd have to see the room first. Bingo!

"I almost lost my shit when this guy in the hardware aisle asked me what size drill bit I was looking for. I had to smile and tell him I can never find one big enough. We were in the bathroom sucking each other off in less than a minute, and he followed me home right after that to that bedroom I still haven't painted yet. It may never get painted!"

Who you can meet: Horny guys shopping for, but never actually buying, home improvement items

What to watch out for: Guys who actually are shopping for nail guns at 2 A.M.

Potential come-ons: "Can you show me how you use that tool?"

DECIDING WHAT YOU REALLY WANT IN BED

4

Refining Your Sex Palate

Your sexual mojo is mighty. It can be as powerful a drive as thirst or hunger. And consequently, your sex drive can get you to do some very stupid things, like going home with the first open orifice that offers you a place to stick your dick. Just as a constant diet of junk food is bad for your bod, repeatedly hooking up with anyone who will take you home (or behind the bushes) is bad for your sex life. Twinkies and potato chips will satisfy your hunger, but they won't do much good for your waistline. By making a little bit of an effort to refine your palate sexually, you can learn to make even quickie sex more enjoyable. We put a lot of effort into getting some action. Why not make the experience as memorable and satisfying as possible?

Getting Over the Slut Syndrome

There was a time in your life—maybe it's even happening right now—when it seemed your every waking moment was consumed with sex. Guys who are in this phase are always thinking about where to get it, who to have it with, who to have it with after that, and how to have it a different way with the next guy. This special time in every fag's life is called a **slutty phase,** and it happens to the best of us. (It's not to be confused with *being a slut,* which isn't such a great thing.)

The slutty phase is a queer developmental stage that often occurs later in gay men than it does in straight men. Straight men get to "play the field" as teens or young adults. But as gay men we often have to repress that part of our sexual development until we're out of our parents' houses and out of the closet. Aside from being a miserable fucking experience, being closeted has the added drawback of retarding that part of our social development that involves dating and sexual relationships—real relationships, not just knowing how your parts fit into his parts. So why do we go through the slutty phase?

Maybe you've made some friends during this phase and you had sex with them. Maybe you met some strangers and you had sex with them too. You met some friends of friends and you had sex with them, and with their boyfriends, and with the cable repairman who came to fix their reception. (You get the picture—especially if you've been there.) But just how do you know if you've experienced that slutty phase—or even if you're in it now? Here are some scenarios that might ring a bell.

Maybe you are fresh out of the closet and just starting to date. Coming out can be a hugely liberating experience, especially if you're liberating yourself from a sexually repressive identity, family, or religion. Engaging in a little butt-love with other guys is not tantamount to cracking open the door to Armageddon. When you've finally convinced yourself of that fact, it becomes clear that the hetero-normative ideal of romantic behavior (boy+girl=valid relationship) doesn't apply to you. It's easy to assume, by taking this concept to its logical extreme, that you can dismiss all conventions about romantic relationships—gay relationships included. You could conceivably just fuck, fuck, fuck to your heart's content, never worrying about tedious details like second dates, arguments with a boyfriend, the drama (and trauma) of moving in together, the frustration of having to negotiate for control of the remote control, etc. The trouble with a philosophy of total sexual liberation is that it can lead to a lot of bad lays.

Maybe you're recently single after years of monogamy and your newfound freedom has energized you with a feeling of liberation. You're in love with the experience of having new lovers, different bodies, different cocks, and a different hot breath on your neck. Maybe you're thrilled to be with someone who doesn't feel so overly comfortable with you that he thinks nothing of clipping his toenails while you're eating dinner, like your last boyfriend used to do. There are a million reasons why emerging from a lackluster love life or an emotionally unsatisfying relationship can send a man right back into slut mode, even if he's been through it before.

Perhaps you just moved from a small town with relatively few hook-up options to the big, gay city, and now you're like a horny kid in a cock-'n'-candy store. As a former midsize-town boy myself, I quickly realized after moving to Los Angeles that I could date or fuck as many guys in a week as I wanted, provided that they didn't know each other. Hallelujah! That was one of the reasons I moved here! And in a big town, I learned that the chances my tricks would know each other were slim—unless they were actors (as though you need another reason not to date actors; there should be a law forcing them to only date one another).

The meat-market forces in a big city create different sexual **homonomics**—gay sexual economics—than they do in a small town. A small population means fewer fuckable options.

This creates low supply and high demand (though for homos, demand is always high). Any Economics 101 student can tell you that if supply is low and demand is high, the relative value of a fuck increases. In a larger city, a higher population means there are more fuckable options—in other words, there's a high supply. Hence, the relative value of a fuck goes way down in the big city. Sex is easier to come by. And cheap, readily available sex is a perfect catalyst for a slutty phase.

There are lots of reasons that slutty behavior might happen, but there are a few obvious problems with it if it persists beyond the typical duration of a year or two. Not the least of these problems is a significantly increased risk of getting an STD. Guys who continue their slutty phase for several years might be suffering from sexual addiction or a fear of intimacy (code for "too fucked up to mess with"). Guys who don't grow out of their slutty phase are in danger of becoming sluts permanently!

Before you complain that I'm moralizing, you should know that I wouldn't dare! The slutty phase is lots of fun, and one can revisit his slutty side *occasionally*. I've done slutty things before and I'm sure there will be opportunities in the future for me to act trashy. I'm a firm believer in gay sexual liberation and the creed that our lives needn't be patterned after rigid, outdated, monogamist, hetero modes of thinking. You should be able to fuck whomever you like (children, animals, and the comatose being obvious exceptions), so long as they want to fuck you too. And we should do it guilt-free.

But there's something to be said for a tiny bit of restraint. Slutty behavior on a daily basis can prevent you from finding the man of your dreams (sluts don't get much respect). It can also keep you from discovering what you really like in bed (how can you know if you want him to play with your nipples when you never get that far in the darkroom at a bar?).

Think about it this way: If you meet a fellow slutty guy for a slutty encounter and have amazing, mind-blowing, sweat-drenched, anonymous monkey love, what are the chances that he'll be around for round two? Slim to none. If you have similar agendas, he'll be looking for his next trick, and most likely he'll assume you're looking for your next trick too. Or perhaps he doesn't even care enough to imagine what you're interested in. Unless you're able to say "Let's figure out how we can do this again," you'll have missed out on more wall-crawling, chandelier-swinging, Tarzan-yodeling sex that might have been.

True sex addiction—a psychological condition—can cause depression, suicidal thoughts, poor self-esteem, shame, self-loathing, despair, anxiety, loneliness, fear of abandonment, and other fun perks. True sex addicts can diagnose their behavior if their escapades lead to shame, deceit, and abuse—and for those men, many treatment options and forms of counseling are readily available and necessary.

Garden-variety sluts can begin modifying their behavior by taking an inventory of the amount of time in a day they spend having sex or searching for or planning for sex. Another behavior modification tactic is to get to know the full names of all your sexual encounters. Anyone who is unwilling to give his real name and engage in a conversation before sex is simply too slutty for you. The idea is to turn from a slut into a stud. How? Read on.

Being Selective

A stud can read the clues that prospective sexual partners give off through their speech, behavior, and body language. Every man drops clues to some of his sexual proclivities, whether he knows he's doing it or not. By closely but surreptitiously observing a potential hookup, you can pick up on the clues that will let you know a little bit more about what he likes in bed.

Clue: He keeps looking over your shoulder when he's talking or flirting with you.
What this means: He's looking for something better to come along.

He may not be a bad guy, but (especially if he's living in a gay ghetto) he may be conditioned to always look for something better, even if you're the best thing he's ever laid eyes on. Or, maybe he's an asshole. Either way, he's not going to give you his full attention. This is known as the *over-the-shoulder syndrome*. Whether you're with him in a crowded gay bar or club (the place where this syndrome is typically cultivated) or any restaurant, fund-raiser, art museum, or other place where eligible men might walk by, he'll continue to check out the guys. In the worst cases of this syndrome your prospective lay won't even give you his full attention when you're in bed together.

Clue: He's pie-eyed, gnashing his teeth, bouncing up and down, and sucking on a lollipop.
What this means: He's *tweaking* hard.

Whether you met him at a circuit party (highly likely), a dance club (somewhat likely), or a bar (occasionally), your new guy pal is high on crystal methamphetamine. Avoid this guy, and if he's already made his way into your bed before your little inner lightbulb goes on (Aha! He's a tweaker!), kick him out immediately and don't invite him back. He probably won't get hard anyway. After a few close encounters with tweakers, you'll be able to spot them at 20 paces and you'll quickly realize why tweakers usually pair up with other tweakers. It's like an insurance policy that their drug-fueled impotence will be mutual, and that no one else will ever hear about it.

Clue: He wears shorty shorts at the gym and spends lots of time on the glute and hamstring machines.
What this means: He's an aggressive bottom.

Whether he's bending over for dumbbells or bending over at the drinking fountain for a bit longer than most other people, his every move and stitch of clothing is designed to enhance his perfect posterior. And he's bending over a lot. All that time on the hamstring machine and doing squats serves a dual function: Not only is he mesmerizing you while you watch him work out, he's also toning and shaping that perfect tush. And he's probably looking for a guy who's willing to give it a good workout—outside of the gym.

Clue: Before he even asks your name, he says, "I'm a total top."

What this means: He has issues with control and masculinity.

He may not want you to ever go near his ass, or he may want you to manhandle him in bed and convince him to bottom, just so he can say, "I've never done this before!"

Clue: He's got a big bulge up front.

What this means: While one might suspect this is the clue that will lead to guys with mammoth members, unfortunately, this is the anti-clue.

There's almost no way to tell how big his cock is going to be when it's hard simply by looking at his package when he's clothed. Caveat emptor! He may be a shower, not a grower, and he may be using a tried and true go-go boy technique: He may be **tied off** or using a cock ring to stay semihard when he's wearing tight pants. Hell, it caught your eye, right? It's not exactly false advertising (true, if he's got a python when he's wearing pants, you'll probably get a python when he drops his drawers), but the marketing promises of the penis can vary greatly from the actual product once it's unwrapped.

Clue: He only pays with credit cards, he won't take you to his apartment, and he has no visible means of employment.

What this means: Either he's a closeted trust-funder living with his parents or—more likely—he's a kept man.

Hookups with kept men can be fun. He's either gorgeous or he's honed his bedroom skills to consummate perfection—after all, someone is probably paying his credit card bill because of his looks or skills in bed. Just don't expect more than a night or two with him. His body—if not his heart—belongs to daddy: sugar daddy.

Clue: He drives a Miata.
What this means: He's a bottom.

How Guys Determine Their Type

It's a common scene in almost any gay environment: Two friends are standing together, watching as other men congregate, chat, walk by. One friend points a guy out to the other and says, "Oh man, he's hot. What do you think?" The other friend responds, "Maybe, but he's not my type at all."

Ask most men how they'd describe a perfect fuck or a fantasy boyfriend and you'll get a list of attributes that describe one man's physical, emotional, or intellectual ideal. Types can be as simple as *tall, dark, and handsome* or as uniquely individual as *an Asian leather daddy with a goatee and a thing for spanking.*

Some men gravitate toward a type as a result of social or cultural influences. For example, some guys prefer men of ethnic groups other than their own because they see those men as more exotic. On the other hand, there are men who won't date outside their ethnic groups at all. Some men only like jocks or men who are under 30 or men who look like fashion models. These preferences for certain types of men are often cultivated and reinforced by TV, magazines, advertising, films, and the other media we consume. While plenty of our preferred types are the result of harmless fantasy, some of our preferences are rooted in our less wholesome assumptions about race, religion, or age.

Some of our types are the result of subconscious psychological factors: Some men prefer dating men older than they are, or men who look just like they do, or men who are "straight-acting." The types can be the manifestation of many subtle influences. Any armchair therapist who has watched *Love Lines* or *Oprah* can spot a person who's after a controlling older man (a father figure) as the result of some childhood daddy drama. Narcissists and insecure guys often search for someone just like themselves. Could it be an unconscious attempt to reassure themselves that they're worth dating? Or maybe it's just about doubling your wardrobe by dating someone with the same tastes and build.

Having a clearly defined type may seem like an asset in your quest to get laid. Your preferences can help determine where the kind of man to whom you're attracted is likely to be found. If, for example, you like young Latino men, it makes sense to go where they gather in abundance—like a club night geared to attract young, gay Latino men. Similarly, if you prefer bears, a leather and Levi's bar or a weekend gathering for bears is a place where you can be sure bears will be plentiful. If you prefer athletes, joining a gay sports team will put you right in the midst of a bunch of eligible jocks. Most large cities—and many midsize ones—have a population large and diverse enough that if a particular ethnic or age group is what gets your motor running, you can easily find places where your type hangs out.

The Trouble With Being Too Picky

There are limitations to dating guys who only fit a certain type. If you believe that your type is the only kind of man to whom you can be attracted, that mindset can be a limiting factor in your sex life. There might be a ton of guys out there who would really get you hot and bothered, but if you're too obsessed with only seeking out one type, you might never encounter them.

It's entirely natural for you to have preferences, but you

shouldn't let a narrow definition of your ideal man get in the way of making a good connection with someone simply because he isn't the kind of person you have in mind. Every relationship of every kind—momentary, temporary, or long-term—gives us the opportunity to learn and expand our horizons in regard to our sex lives. The fewer your limitations on your prospects for sexual connection, the greater your options are.

As Woody Allen famously said, "Being bisexual doubles your chance of a date on Saturday night." It's a bit of an over-statement, but the point remains: Having more types increases your chances of getting lucky. Just like being too eager to jump into the sack with any Tom or Hairy Dick, being too picky can ruin your chances for a good time too.

If this book were called *How to Fuck Indiscriminately*, it would be a very short book, so before saying that we shouldn't be picky about whom we hook up with, let's acknowledge that we should all be selective when it comes to sex. At the same time, if you are constantly telling yourself and other people that you're picky, and that you're not getting laid because you are so picky, then one of three things is likely happening:

1) You may have an exaggerated sense of your own attractiveness or eligibility, and you feel that there are no suitable matches for your charm, good looks, prowess in the sack, and general studliness. In other words, you're a vain prick. Go on telling people how picky you are and eventually some other equally picky guy will come your way. Either he will reject your advances and bruise your ego because he's even more vain than you are and, not surprisingly, he'll assume you're a vain prick. Or he'll hook up with you and you'll make a great self-absorbed pair until one or both of you decides you are too good for the other one. (And sex between vain people is the most boring sex on earth.)

2) You really *are* better than most of the other guys around. This is an acceptable excuse for not hooking up in the following locations: offshore oil rigs, Dungeons and Dragons conventions, and Celine Dion concerts.

3) You're using your pickiness as a way to avoid being intimate with another guy, or out of fear of rejection.

If your problem is number 1, then check the ego, buddy. You are no fun to be around, and the rest of us would all rather you just not show up to the party (and ruin our good time) until you can act a little more human. Go on and be hot. Hot is good. But telling us you're *too* hot for us mere mortals is just sad for you, because you won't be hot forever. Then you'll be *formerly* hot and totally alone.

If your pickiness is due to problem number 2—you really are too good for the guys around you—then consider changing where you're hanging out. You'll find some tips on finding a more suitable location for hooking up in chapter three.

If your pickiness is related to problem number 3—your standards are keeping you from meeting decent guys—you need to reassess your impossibly high standards. It's not the other guys who are really the problem.

It's easy to say that there's something about a potential hookup (or even a potential boyfriend) that you deem substandard. Maybe his fashion sense isn't as sophisticated as yours. Maybe he likes fruity cocktails and you prefer a manlier drink like whisky or beer. Maybe he talks about work, or sports, or his mom too much. Maybe he's a sweet, sexy guy whose purse falls out when he opens his mouth. If you're finding that no man ever meets your unattainable ideals, then you'll never meet a guy and have any kind of bad experience—in bed or in a relationship. You'll never have a mediocre romp in the sack, you'll never fall in love with a guy who isn't good for you, and you'll never have your heart broken, either.

You'll still be able to constantly complain that all the good guys are taken, or that all the smart guys are ugly, or that all the hot guys are jerks, or that only bears or queens or Republicans are into you, or whatever. Rejecting everyone before they can reject you is the simplest way to not be disappointed by other men, and simultaneously to be constantly disappointed by them. But what it won't do is get you laid.

No guy is perfect. But if you dismiss a guy too quickly, you'll never know when you've met the perfect guy for you because you'll never give anyone enough opportunity to show you.

So how do you drop the irrational pickiness? Here a few pointers:

• A little confidence building is usually a good place to start. Take a personal inventory of your strengths and weaknesses. Write down all the reasons that you're a great catch. Yeah, the idea is a little crunchy, but think about what you've got to offer your dream man, and not just what he's got to offer you. Get a little bit Stuart Smalley on yourself. You *are* good enough, doggone it! But if you don't think you're worth it, chances are a potential hookup won't either. Your lack of self-confidence will be visible on your face and in your demeanor, and it's *so* not sexy to be down on yourself.

• Be more realistic with your standards. If you live in the Castro and you refuse to date a circuit queen, so be it; there are plenty other guys to choose from. But if you live in Laguna Beach and you don't want to date surfer dudes or gay tourists, you're going to have a hard time scoring since you've instantly rejected most of your prospects. Outside of surfers and gay tourists, there's not much left in Laguna.

• Take a good, hard look at your prejudices. You say you won't date surfers or gay tourists? Why not? Do you have enough information about surfers to justifiably put the kibosh

on *all* of them? What about tourists? If you've ever vacationed before, then *you* were a gay tourist. They can't all be bad— you were once one of them yourself. The more you learn about people, the fewer your prejudices will be. So make sure you think critically about your prejudices before hastily dismissing someone.

• Risk getting your ego bruised occasionally. Go up to someone who interests you and say hi. If you put your foot in your mouth or if he is clearly uninterested, your pride might be wounded temporarily, but sure as the sun will rise tomorrow, there will be other opportunities and other guys. Work on developing a thicker skin. Then go up to the next guy and say hi.

Myth vs. Fact

There are lies (*I'm an astronaut...I'll introduce you to David Geffen... I can go for four hours at a time... I'm a total top...*) and there are myths. Lies are the things guys will say to get sex. Myths are fictions or half-truths, and in the world of sexual relations, myths will get you into far more trouble than you're looking for. Even guys who have been around the block a few times often lack some basic information about sex; instead, they rely on some widely held myths that are usually a load of crap. Operating your equipment with a crappy owner's manual is simply no good. But having a working knowledge of the myths surrounding gay sex—and the information that debunks the myths—will improve your overall sexual experience.

Myth: Sex should always be great.
Fact: Sometimes it's not. That's no reason not to try it again. And again.

Myth: You should always have an orgasm.
Fact: If you are healthy, you'll probably have an orgasm most of the time you have sex. If you or your butt buddy don't blow your wad during sex occasionally, don't sweat it. It can happen to healthy, virile guys sometimes.

Myth: Your cock should always get hard and always stay hard as long as you're aroused or having sex.
Fact: Some guys stay rock-hard for hours. Some guys go up and

down. Some guys don't stay erect when they're getting fucked. This doesn't necessarily mean they're not aroused or having a hot time. One can be simultaneously aroused and not hard.

Myth: You should never pass up sex.
Fact: Chances are good that if you pass up a fuck, you'll have another shot at sex sooner or later. If your immediate prospects aren't all that enticing, you can always go home and get yourself off. Consider which is worse: Passing up a chance to tea-bag a guy you'll later wish you hadn't (like your boss or your ex or your best friend's boyfriend) or just going home for a little solo batting practice.

Myth: Safe sex is boring sex.
Fact: Boring sex is boring sex. Safe sex can be as hot as any sex. Your job (with my help) is to make safe sex sexy. But whining about using condoms will definitely make for lousy sex.

Myth: If you're not fucking, it's not really sex.
Fact: This is a question of semantics, really. Ultimately, who cares what it's called? Everyone has a different definition of sex, but my rule of thumb is this: If you're naked in the company of another person (or people) and you're involved in an act that induces an orgasm, it's probably sex. But really, why get hung up on what someone else calls it?

Myth: The size of your dick is an indication of the strength of your libido.
Fact: You can be hung like an elephant and be as sexually listless as a sloth, or you could be hung like a hamster and have the sex drive of a jackrabbit. (Where did all these animal metaphors come from?) There is no correlation between dick size and sex drive.

Myth: The larger your cock, the greater the stimulation for your partner during intercourse.

Fact: Big dicks can be a visual turn-on for size queens, but a big one is not a guarantee of increased stimulation. Big or small, you have to know how to use what you've got. Besides, your dick isn't the only tool you have. You've got fingers, a tongue, lips, and a whole bunch of other parts that you can use to provide stimulation.

Myth: Your sexuality peaks during adolescence. After the age of 20, your sexual ability, interest, and enjoyment of sex decline.

Fact: While you may not be able to pop off eight times in a day when you're 40 (but mazel tov if you can!), there's no reason you can't be better at sex than you were at 20. As for levels of sexual interest, try telling the dirty old man who hangs out at my local gay bookstore, leering at everything in pants, that because he's, like, 70 his interest in sex should have dropped off by now. And enjoyment? Most sexually active older people report that sex continues to get better (if not more frequent) throughout their lives, even into ripe old age.

Myth: It's natural for you to be chiefly interested in intercourse and orgasm. Foreplay and affectionate touching are not part of "real" sex.

Fact: Sex doesn't follow a strict recipe or a series of steps written in stone. If you and your partner(s) are interested in what's going on between you, then you're doing it right. (Quite literally, foreplay is for girls. Women and men have different modes and levels of arousal, which makes foreplay in hetero pairings essential to get the woman "ready." Foreplay as it's conventionally defined has little to do with preparing gay men for sexual contact.)

Myth: If you're unable to maintain an erection even once, you'll likely develop a major sex problem.
Fact: An occasional bout of impotence is normal and common and is not necessarily an indicator of future sexual dysfunction.

Myth: The success of your first experience with intercourse is an indicator of how successful you will be during the rest of your sexual life.
Fact: Many gay men are proverbial ugly ducklings when it comes to sex and often turn out to be sexual tigers after picking up a tip or two—and a little practice. Plenty of us had our first sexual experiences with women, and that wasn't an indicator of heterosexuality!

Myth: A preference for oral sex is a sign of immaturity.
Fact: Blasphemy! Gay men love oral sex, generally speaking, and some perfectly mature men prefer going down to other varieties of sex.

Myth: Masturbation is bad for you.
Fact: There's a test for this one: Put down this book right now, go rub one out, then come back before you read on. If you die or become horribly disfigured or develop a nasty rash on the way back to your reading nook, then the myth is true. If not, jerk off to your heart's content. Totally abstaining from masturbation is more likely to cause your body harm than yanking your doodle dandy.

Myth: A healthy well-adjusted man should have no trouble performing sexually in any situation.
Fact: Stress, booze, and many party drugs can all contribute to a less than stellar performance in bed. Plenty of well-

adjusted guys overindulge at times, or get a little too stressed to put on a good show.

Myth: Erection is always a sign of sexual excitement and indicates a need for intercourse.
Fact: Erections often indicate arousal, but they can also happen spontaneously without arousal—like morning wood. Besides, as much as you may want sex, there's no such thing as a physiological need for intercourse.

Myth: Some men are naturally better lovers than others. While you may be able to learn certain sexual skills, you will never be able to match the performance of someone who has a greater inborn ability.
Fact: Like natural athletic ability, some guys take to sex more easily than others. But with practice and a little know-how, anyone can improve his game.

Myth: Simultaneous orgasm is the most fulfilling sexual goal.
Fact: Simultaneous orgasm can be nice, but watching him shoot, then having him watch you shoot, can be just as pleasurable. Getting hung up on simultaneous orgasm is a colossal waste of energy.

Myth: When a man reaches adulthood, he loses interest in fantasy and masturbation and concentrates exclusively on intercourse.
Fact: Honking your horn at any age is fun. Adulthood has no impact on the fun of fantasy and masturbation, and there's nothing immature about jerkin' the gherkin.

Myth: Republicans are lousy lays.
Fact: This one, I'm afraid, is absolutely true.

Feel like you've been lied to all your life? It's my privilege to provide you with some honest-to-gosh truths about sex that you can believe.

Fun Facts About Sex

• The first acts of sexual intercourse took place about 1 1/2 billion years ago, when two creatures of the same species first swapped DNA. And it's just been getting hotter ever since.

• Your testosterone levels are highest at dawn, but sex most often occurs in the evening. Why? I don't know. But it's a good excuse to work out that morning wood.

• Oxytocin—the brain chemical that floods the body during sex, leading to feelings of pleasure, altruism, calm, bonding, and satisfaction—also floods through a mother and baby during childbirth to promote the bonding experience. So falling for the guy who's blowing you is just another sparkle in the beautiful kaleidoscope of nature.

• The speed of seminal fluid during ejaculation has been measured at 28 mph, though it does slow down when it passes through the penis. Cover your eyes!

But seriously, folks, without knowing the facts about the sexual situations we find ourselves in, we run the risk of getting caught up in silly (and sometimes dangerous) half-truths and preconceived notions of how sex is supposed to go. It's easy to be disappointed when things don't go as we expect them to, but maybe those expectations are based on myth. Say the guy whose butt you're burgling doesn't have a hard dick when he's getting fucked. You might assume he's not aroused. The truth of the matter is that it happens to lots of guys, and it doesn't mean he's not aroused. Likewise, getting wrapped up in ridiculous ideas like masturbating being for adolescents, or that you and your partner must have simultaneous orgasms, is simply fruitless, my dear fruits.

5 A SAFE BET

Whatever you think you know about making your sex life safe, it's not enough. Denial ain't just a river in Egypt. Sadly, it's a fact of life in this country for lots of people who engage in sex. The plain truth is that as long as you're having sex, you're exposing yourself to various kinds of risk. As long as there are sexually transmitted diseases (STDs), sex will involve taking some chances.

Listen: It's no fun, but you've got to know this stuff, dearies. Your health is on the line.

Sex is about playing the odds. Unless you have sex with only one particular person (namely, yourself) you'll very likely be exposed to STDs sooner or later. If you've ever had sex, you've probably already been exposed, with or without your knowing it. So get comfortable and read this chapter all the way through, because knowing a thing or two about reducing your risks can go a long way in making sure you get to have sex throughout your whole, long, healthy life.

Since the idea of telling unmarried people to "just say no" to sex (and hoping unwanted pregnancy and STDs will simply go away) hasn't quite worked out the way conservative Republican administrations might've liked (primarily because it's a half-baked, lame-brained, self-righteous, patently stupid idea), I'll not advocate abstinence. It works for some people, but not for me. If you're going to have sex—and I'm all for your having sex—then you need to know how to do it safely.

STDs in the USA

Here's a sad little fact: The United States has the highest rates of STDs of any industrialized nation. Just why is that the case? For starters, instead of *useful* knowledge and condoms, we're passing out shame and stigma when it comes to sex. Most of the states in the good ol' USA generally take a backward, puritanical approach to sex education. The *no sex education in schools, please, we're religious* crap clearly doesn't work the way Pat Robertson wants it to.

Remarkably, there are many places in the world where sensible sex education and mature, less repressive sexual attitudes have reduced the rates of transmission for STDs. A trip across the border or across the pond will take you to happy homo paradises like Toronto or Paris or Berlin, where kids are educated about sex, billboards and posters extol the virtues of condoms, and everyone still gets his freak on. *A lot.*

Call me preachy if you like. More important than what you think of my attitude on the subject is the inescapable fact that the more you know, the better equipped you'll be to make conscientious, responsible decisions about sex. You can engage in risk or not: That's your choice. But it's totally irresponsible not to know the consequences of unsafe activities and behavior for your health and for the health of your partners. Once you know enough about sex to make informed choices and decisions, the quality of your experience can only increase.

Very few sexual activities are totally risk-free. Masturbating alone, cyber sex, and no-touch circle jerks are the safest activities. Nearly everything else—including kissing, which carries some chance of hepatitis and herpes transmission—has some degree of risk.

The ugly truth about STDs is that most of them have no visible symptoms, so just because you're not itching or burning or breaking out, that doesn't mean you're in the clear. Also, having one STD doesn't mean you can't get another. If you do get two or more infections, they can compound their effects, making each condition nastier than it was before. On top of that, your chances of contracting HIV—the biggie— increase if you're already infected with another STD. Some diseases, like chlamydia, can be cleared up with some readily available medication. Some, like herpes, stay with you for life. The. Rest. Of. Your. Life.

Fun stuff, huh? Stop kidding yourself and get tested already.

It's true that none of this totally unsexy information will help you score. Why am I schooling you on this? Because chances are that your high school health teacher probably never did—or wasn't allowed to. But when it comes to getting laid, scoring successfully also means being smart.

The List

Here's a quickie primer on STDs—the most infamous ones, at least. For more complete information go to the Centers for Disease Control and Prevention Web site at *www.cdc.gov* or give their STD hotline a call at (800) 227-8922.

Herpes: About one in five Americans has herpes, the virus that causes small blisters on the mouth, lips, eyes, face, or genitals. It comes in two varieties: simplex 1 (HSV-1), which shows up most often on or around the face, and simplex 2 (HSV-2), which usually appears downtown (on your cock, balls, anus, or perineum). Thanks to our natural enthusiasm for oral sex, the two varieties of herpes can swap places occasionally. Once you get herpes—usually when one of your mucous membranes (eyes, anus, urethral opening, mouth) touches one of his open sores—the herpes virus sets up camp in the nerve endings in your spine and never, ever, goes away. Welcome to the H Club! Membership is free and it lasts a lifetime. The virus lies dormant for a while then pops up at the most inopportune moments—as if there's ever a good time for crusty sores. There's no cure or preventative medicine, but you can tame the H beast with prescription medications that will help keep outbreaks minimal and reduce the chances that you'll give someone else the gift that keeps on giving. Call the lovely folks at the National Herpes Hotline at (919) 361-8488 or go to www.ashastd.org/hrc for the lowdown on the sores, the treatments, and support chat. You can even sign up for a HerpesNet e-mail account. (Don't send e-mail to your mom from that account.)

Gonorrhea: It's the one that's been around the longest, and it's got the cutest little nicknames (the dose, the clap, the drip). Spread through unprotected sex, it's a bacterial infection that causes a puslike discharge from your urethra—the little hole at the end of your dick. As if having a discharge from your pee hole weren't fun enough, the clap makes every trip to the urinal feel like you're pissing fire. Luckily, the cure is simple: a single treatment of an antibiotic for you and your partners and no sex for a week. Yes, you should tell your partners and get them treated so they don't give it back to you after you've been cleared up. And you don't want to deal with the nasty complications that arise if you let it go untreated. Plenty of people who have it never show symptoms, so when you have your yearly physical, be sure to get an STD screening.

Chlamydia: It's a popular one among the under-25 set. Though it sounds like the name of a pretty flower, it's actually a bacterial infection that can cause infertility. It will wreak havoc on your penis, anus, throat, and eyes if you let it, but it's a quiet, sneaky bugger, and it's the STD least likely to stomp around your body shouting out symptoms. It's spread just like gonorrhea—through unprotected anal and vaginal intercourse, oral sex, and sharing sex toys. You can cure it just like you cure the clap: by going to a doctor or a clinic for antibiotics.

Scabies and pubic lice (crabs): These are two varieties of little parasites that cause nasty, itchy skin conditions. The little invaders love the warmth of your groin and other hairy parts. Crabs are itty-bitty vampires that bite your skin and feed on your blood. Scabies burrow under your skin, lay eggs, and excrete waste and other fun things. Both infestations will cause you to itch like a motherfucker. Crabs can be spread through sexual contact or in bedding, clothing, and upholstered furniture—all of which you'll have to thoroughly clean after you treat the condition on your body. Scabies are spread by skin-to-skin contact. For crabs, a simple over-the-counter shampoo will get rid of the unwelcome visitors. To get scabies medication you'll need a prescription.

Hepatitis: All varieties of this nasty viral infection are diseases that affect the liver. A few are more commonly associated with sex. You get hepatitis A by ingesting contaminated poo (it happens!), and it causes flu-like symptoms. With bed rest and an injection of immunoglobulin, most people kick the disease within six months and are thereafter immune from getting it again and from spreading it. Hepatitis B is the variety that's more often sexually transmitted (through unprotected anal, vaginal, and oral sex). It causes flu-like symptoms, hives, dark-colored urine, and abdominal and joint pain. It's preventable and treatable, and—like hep A—once you recover from it, you won't get it again. For either variety, you'll definitely need your doc's help. The consequences of going untreated are deadly.

Human papillomavirus (HPV): HPV is a viral infection—and viral STDs have no cure. HPV comes in more varieties than Baskin-Robbins ice cream, it's supercontagious, and it may stick with you for life (or it may just clear up and scoot along). It's very common, very hard to detect (especially if you don't have symptoms), and totally impossible to track. The disease causes little warts on your dick, balls, anus, or inside your ass. Most gay men who engage in anal sex will contract HPV eventually, but it's not usually a dangerous disease by itself. HPV is linked to increased chances of getting certain types of cancer—most often cervical cancer in women. The risk of men developing penile or anal cancer is low, although it is possible. Your immune system might cause the warts to disappear after about six months, or you can have them treated (freezing, cutting, lasering, or burning them off, even in the butt) to reduce your chances of passing them on to others. Guys are almost never examined for HPV even when they ask for the STD screenings, so if you've been with someone you know has had it, be specific and ask for an HPV screening. Cigarette smokers get more warts—as if you needed another reason to quit smoking.

Syphilis: This treatable bacterial disease had been on the decline in the United States until recently, but it's trying to make a comeback with homos in big cities. It's still totally possible to eradicate the disease, like we did with that sono-fabitch polio, but only if we all work together. Syphilis starts with painless little ulcers or sores on the genitals, anus, lips, or even the fingertips, and gets progressively worse from there—a lot worse. A little penicillin can kick syphilis, but if you continue to have sex with the person you got it from, he's got to get the penicillin too or he'll just keep giving it back to you like you're playing a game of STD ping-pong. If you don't treat it, you can look forward to disfigurement, insanity, blindness, neurological disorders, and death. So treat it, for cryin' out loud!

HIV/AIDS: This one is the biggie. Human immunodeficiency virus (HIV) is the communicable disease that you can get through contact with blood, semen, vaginal fluid, or breast milk. The average amount of time before you start showing symptoms after contracting HIV is 10 years, but you're contagious from the moment you get it. HIV shreds your immune system, leading to acquired immune deficiency syndrome (AIDS). AIDS leaves your body susceptible to all kinds of diseases that can actually do you in, like pneumonia, cancer, and a common killer of AIDS patients—tuberculosis. HIV/AIDS decimated the gay community in the '80s and '90s, and even today—after all the AIDS-related Broadway musicals and tear-jerker Oscar-winning movies (starring straight people!)—straight and gay people are still getting it all the time. In America about 40,000 new infections occur each year. Treatments are improving, and many people are now living with HIV/AIDS rather than dying from it. But the treatments are complicated, have serious side effects, and are very expensive. For information on HIV/AIDS go online to amfAR.org, a good source of information. Everything you'll find, of course, is stuff you should already know. But too many of us have been lulled into a false sense of security about AIDS. Yes, you can still get it, and yes, you may still die from it. There's no cure and you have to play safe because there is absolutely no way to tell if someone has HIV by looking at him. Don't assume any sex partner is HIV-negative.

Condoms

Condoms provide very good protection against the transmission of many STDs. If you didn't already know this fact—perhaps because you were born and raised in a sealed underground bomb shelter—then consider yourself informed now. With regard to HIV in particular, correct condom use will lessen the risk of transmission by a factor of up to 10,000. The best ways to play it safe are to learn to use condoms properly, be a little bit choosy about whom you fuck, and educate yourself on lower-risk behaviors (oral sex, mutual masturbation) should you end up in bed with someone you're not sure is STD-free.

So You've Got a Social Disease

Condoms aren't the perfect solution, so if you've gone and gotten yourself a social disease, don't beat yourself up over it. You're not an unlovable diseased slut pariah. Plenty of people get STDs—in fact, about one in three sexually active people get some form of STD by age 24.

If you think you've been exposed to an STD—if you've got sores on your asshole or your balls, or if it burns when you pee—then get thee to a physician right away. Like, *now*. If you don't think your physician is particularly gay-friendly, then go to a health clinic. Your pesky new STD friend probably won't go away by itself, and wishing it away upon a star only works for the Blue Fairy—not you, fairy. Even if your symptoms go away, that doesn't necessarily mean you're home free. Some diseases like to lie low and simmer in your body while you spread them to lots of other people, then they creep back to the surface and attack your vital organs, immune system, and precious family jewels with a vengeance. Masturbating won't make you go blind or insane, but syphilis will, so the least you can do is find out if you've got it.

More important than knowing how you got your STD is getting yourself tested and not behaving like an asshole after you know you have it. If you're being treated, then don't go fucking around with anyone *until you're no longer infectious.* Not sure if you're infectious? Then ask your damn doctor. If you've got a disease that will be around for the long haul, like HIV or herpes, then you must inform your partners of the risks of transmission before you engage in any activity that might pass on the disease. By the way, no disease means the end of your sex life. But if you don't tell your partners, then you're officially a rotten person and may your dick shrivel up and fall off. Don't fuck around with other people's health. Seriously.

When He Won't Wrap His Willy

You know why you need condoms—now you need to use them. They're not expensive (about $1 each) and they come in a variety of pretty colors, textures, flavors, and materials.

Some guys prefer barebacking. The reason for their preference may be (a) they're HIV-positive and unaware that they can contract different, more drug-resistant strains of the disease through unprotected sex, making treatment tougher; (b) they don't believe HIV causes AIDS—it's a ridiculous conspiracy theory (if that's his reason for not wrapping it up, then you're not just dealing with a jerk but a crackpot too); or (c) they're simpletons, bug chasers, or they've been living in a cave in Bhutan since 1981 and they're unaware of the need for protection. Some guys will give you a bunch of sanctimonious guff about how condoms are a hassle, they're uncomfortable, they're deal-breakers, etc. These people are a part of the problem. You don't have to be.

You already know you need to use condoms, so you've got a few choices when it comes to getting a reluctant partner to use them during sex. If he won't use a condom:

• **Make it feel good.** Not all condoms are constrictive. Some are shaped with a balloon top to give extra sensation at the head of the penis. Condoms don't have to reduce sensation. Get some that are designed to promote good friction. Make sure he knows the options, or no nookie.

• **Teach him to love condoms by making safe sex hot.** While you're in the throes of passion, stare him straight in the eye, tear open the condom wrapper, and wrap his sausage (or yours). Put a new, unwrapped condom in your mouth and slowly roll it onto his dick with your lips and tongue without using your hands. A practice session with a banana is all you'll need to perfect the technique. Sizzling! Jimmy hats don't have to be clinical to be safe. If you think it's sexy, he will too.

• **Keep a few different sizes on hand.** If you don't know what kind fits you best, go buy a few packs and experiment until you find one that fits you well and feels good. Masturbate with water-based or silicone-based lube while you're wearing a latex or polyurethane condom to get a sense of which ones feel best. Jerking with a rubber on will get you accustomed to the feeling of wearing one, and it makes solo-sex cleanups a snap. After you learn to apply the techniques in this book, you'll be bringing home a wide assortment of hotties, so you'll need to have a few different sizes of condoms on hand to make sure you've got the right fit for Mr. Right Now. Condoms labeled "snug" and "fit" are made for guys on the smaller end of the penile spectrum, and "large" or "magnum" models are designed for the big boys. You don't have to tell him you're using a "snug" condom, but if either of you needs it, use it. If a rubber is too loose, it will slide off and won't be effective in STD prevention. Better-fitting condoms feel better too. If it fits, he will come.

• **_No glove, no love._** Tell him it's your way or the highway. It's as simple as that for you, right? He may be hot, but as you well know, you can't tell if he has HIV or another STD simply by looking at him. He may not even know his HIV status. If he wants your ass or your cock, then you have to insist on a few simple ground rules—and let him know you're not interested in backing down. Don't compromise with your body.

• **_Kick him out of bed._** Use both feet if you have to. If he won't use a condom, then you're done with him. You can always jerk off once the jerk is out the door.

Condoms come in lambskin (never use these—they don't protect against HIV), latex, and polyurethane varieties. Some people are allergic to latex, so rather than giving up on condoms, look for the hypoallergenic polyurethane kind. Condoms come lubed, nonlubed, or lubed with a spermicide. The spermicide variety is no good for gay boys. Nonoxynol-9—the spermicide most often used on condoms—has been shown to kill HIV in the test tube, but it can do more harm than good by irritating the rectal lining, making the bottom guy more likely to contract HIV.

MAKING THE BEST OF BAD SITUATIONS

6

Not every encounter can be the stuff of romance novels. Personally, I'm still waiting for the gay romance novels to show up on supermarket shelves next to the hetero ones—but with Johnny Hazzard on the cover in place of Fabio. But I digress. Since our sex lives can be stranger than fiction, you've got to be prepared to take matters into your own hands if your hookup doesn't go according to plan.

You never know when something unforeseen could happen—or not happen—like you'd hoped. Maybe his equipment is smaller than you were anticipating, or maybe your beer goggles are wearing off just about the time you're piling your clothes in a heap at the foot of his bed.

In the next few pages you'll find some clever tips for dealing with problems that are solvable, turning a bad situation around before it's too late, and beating a hasty retreat if there's no alternative.

What to Do When You Can't Get it Up

No amount of me—or anyone else—telling you that it happens sometimes will make its having happened a less embarrassing situation. Nevertheless: It happens sometimes. It's true. Occasional impotence can happen to any guy, young or old, both to guys who run hot and guys who run cool. But imagine you finally get that humpy guy you've been lusting after for a year home to your place and all you want to do is raise the drawbridge...and nothing happens. Argh! If he's hoping for a nice hard salami and your business flops out of your boxers like overcooked linguine, you will be embarrassed. But it's not an irreparable situation.

Cause number 1 for your floppy fella is that you're either too high or too drunk to keep it up. Booze and drugs (including some prescription drugs) can drain the battery power from your Eveready. What to do? Try wearing a cock ring to stiffen your dick, or wait until you're sober and try getting stiff again. If you're high, it all depends on the effects of whatever pill you popped or dust you snorted. Reconvene the fuckfest after you've come down and recovered a bit. If you're drunk, drink lots of water to ward off a hangover. If he's as drunk as you are, then prepare to pass out in each other's arms. In the morning you can wake up, pop a few aspirin, gargle a bit of mouthwash (please!), and get down to the business of getting down.

Cause number 2 could be psychological. Apart from the dick-softening effects of intoxicants like booze and pills, impotence—if you're not yet middle-aged or elderly—is nearly always psychological rather than physical. In other words, it's all in your head. You can psyche yourself out of an erection if you're stressed out, too ill, or if you're feeling some garden-variety performance anxiety (yes, we gays get it too). What do you do? Put on a cock ring to try to boost your hard-on, or just take a few minutes and relax.

Will he wonder why you're taking a time-out when the game is just starting? Maybe. Just tell him you're a little wound up and you need a minute or two to get back into the zone. In the meantime, you can take care of his hard-on for a few minutes, making sure you aren't concentrating on your cock. Worrying about your dick will only compound the problem.

Cause number 3 is physical. If you experience only occasional impotence, and if you're still getting hard-ons in your sleep or morning wood, your erectile difficulty is likely due to one of the first two causes. But if you're having physical problems getting hard—due to obesity, diabetes, or the use of a prescribed medication—you may want to talk to your doctor about alternatives like Viagra. Make an appointment with your physician and get a thorough physical exam (including blood tests), or get a referral to an urologist. If there's no physical problem, then consider talking to a therapist with experience in sexual dysfunction.

Object lesson: Relax. It will help you put the starch back in your shorts.

What to Do When He Can't Get it Up

If you've just read the information above, you have a pretty good sense of what a momentary bout of impotence can do to your psyche. If you're hard as a rock and he's the one with the limp noodle, the worst thing you can do at that moment is stomp his ego by quizzing him on his flaccidity, or get huffy about how you'd hoped he would be able to fuck you to next Tuesday.

Assuming that you don't have any Viagra on hand, you can offer him a cock ring (as you can see, they're remarkably useful little things for just this sort of situation) or try to relax him. If he's just stressed out or if he has performance anxiety, then as soon as he's relaxed and feeling more comfortable, his pocket rocket will rise once again.

One relaxation technique is to have him lie back and not let him do anything to you while you tease his balls with your tongue. You could also put his soft cock in your mouth and gently roll it around (nothing vigorous at this point—that could spook him), play with his ass, or maybe rim him—just let him know you're not disappointed and that the sex can still continue. If that makes him uncomfortable—he may feel like he's on display—then let him go down on you. Servicing you might heat him up and relax him by taking the focus off his cock for a bit.

Whatever you do, don't start saying, "What's the matter? Aren't you into me?" or "Come on, man!" That's not going to get anyone hard.

Object lesson: Never ridicule Mr. Floppy. It could happen to you!

What to Do When You Realize He's the Creature From the Homo Lagoon

First, a word of preemptive advice: If you meet a guy in a dark club or in an alley behind the club or in the steam room at a bathhouse—any dark place—before you promise to take him home for some sexy spelunking in his pleasure cave, drag him into the light so you'll know exactly whom you're enticing with your masculine wiles. He may be more Mr. Hyde than Dr. Jekyll.

But say it's too late for that. You've sobered up after an all-night fling or you finally get a good look at him after making out in a dark club—and he's not what you had imagined or remembered, much to your horror. What do you do?

If he's a couple of steps lower on the evolutionary chart than you usually care to shtup, you have two options that will allow you to politely excuse yourself from bumping uglies (*again,* if you already have) with an ugly: You can escape, or you can turn him off so that *he'll* want to escape.

If you'd prefer to be the one doing the running, just do some warm-up stretches, then politely excuse yourself to go to the bathroom, never to return. Or go "check on" your friends on the other side of the bar or club, or answer that phantom cell phone call. I'm usually loathe to use a cell phone as an excuse for anything, but it may be easier on his feelings than saying, "I'm just now realizing how ass-lick ugly you are and I'd rather not be seen with you, much less allow you into my secret garden." If you prefer a more direct approach, look him in the eye and just tell him, "It was nice [talking with you / making out / fingering each other's butts in the back room] but I've got to get going. Have a great night." He may appreciate your directness. Normally, it would be bad form if after you ditched him he saw you playing grab-ass with another man or if he saw you walk out of the bar with your hands down the back of another guy's pants. Then again, romances are not often made in a dark room, so do as you please.

If you want *him* to hit the road, there are three basic approaches—and all of them require a fair amount of trickery (so save them for dire situations). The first approach is to act as though you think nothing's wrong while indicating nonverbally that something clearly is. Start scratching your crotch like you've got an itchy rash. When he asks, tell him nonchalantly that no one is sure what's wrong but a team of specialists is monitoring your condition and that if he's feeling adventurous, then you're up for a round of train-and-tunnel. Guys don't often stick around after an invitation like that. The second man-repellant involves behaving as though you want something very different from what he wants, sexually speaking. If you can tell he's a bit prudish, you can ask him if he's into a three-way with the next closest guy at the bar. This approach is only useful on prudes: Beware. He might say yes! The third option is the gross-out: Turn him off by mentioning that your meal at the nearby Mexican restaurant isn't sitting well, that your enchilada platter with extra chilies is knocking on your back door.

If you've got some inch-thick beer glasses on after a tankard or two of the local tavern's finest $2 ale, you might take your altered state as a good opportunity to get a second, slightly less drunk opinion from a friend. Ask him whether your new conquest is more Dean Martin or Jerry Lewis. If you're going stag, or if you're not in a place where one might typically take a pal (bathhouse, back alley, truck stop), then you'll just have to trust your own judgment, impaired as it might be. Clearly, it's better not to be inebriated when you're prowling alone.

If after a night of frivolity and/or fucking you wake up from a restful sleep to find that a nightmare is still in your bed and passed out on your arm, your first instinct may be to chew off your limb like a fox caught in a trap. Or you can wait until he wakes up and then quickly shoo him out of your place. It's preferable (and definitely essential in non-inebriated situations) for you to establish the sleepover rules before you get naked (see chapter eight for overnight etiquette), but you're past all that now. Telling him you've got a brunch date is a reasonable excuse for any socially active fag on a weekend. If you went hog wild in the bed of a stranger on a school night, then an early-morning "work meeting" ought to clear the unwanted visitor from your abode.

Object lesson: If making bad decisions about potential bed buddies is a common occurrence for you after a cocktail or three, you should always keep a cab company's number pre-programmed into your cell phone and enough cab fare to get you home if you wake up in unfamiliar territory.

What to Do When the Boyfriends in Your Three-way Start Fighting

If you take a survey of sexually liberated gay men, many of them will tell you that the ménage à trois is the birthright of the homosexual. But say you've bitten off more than you can suck by going off with a pair of guys who seemed sexy and cool at your friend's cocktail party where you met them, but who reveal themselves to be a pair of argumentative drama queens at home.

There should be no confusion about the purpose of going home with a couple—it's all about getting naked and getting it on. The frolicking might start easily enough, with the two of them worshipping every inch of your body, or fulfilling your fantasy of having two cocks to contend with at once, or with you as the **Lucky Pierre** with your dick in one butt while the third's cock is in your ass. But say you—accidentally, of course—pay more attention to one of the guys, or one of them takes a particular liking to you and ignores his hubby. You may soon have a classic hissy fit on your hands.

As absurd as it may be to watch the two of them argue (especially if they're still naked and erect), you can try to defuse the unpleasantly escalating situation by attempting to redirect the focus toward you, or you can retrieve your pants and beat a hasty retreat.

How do you know which route to take? First, you must always play Mr. Neutral Switzerland in an argument between couples if you hope to get any booty before you have to hit the pavement. If the conflict stems from one guy's feeling neglected, then you may be able to calm him down with a few well-placed licks, spanks, and dirty talk. Voilà! You're off to the races again. If he's still not soothed, offer the grumpy Gus a crack at your ass, or a slurp on your cock, or whatever he's itching for.

If he can't be assuaged, or if the greedy one still has a mouthful of your cock while his partner is bitching at him—and he won't let go—then get up, grab your pants, and head for the door. This may be a situation where the couple hasn't worked out their ground rules when they should have. A hot ménage à trois isn't worth the guilt of knowing you were there when a pair split up. If they part ways, you could be branded a home wrecker, even if you were just a (mostly) innocent bystander.

Object lesson: If you're the third, only play with couples you're not likely to run into at another cocktail party the following weekend.

What to Do When You've Got internet Shortsightedness

Speaking of ordering sex in, you must be wary of ordering out for some young guy via the Internet. Sure, chat rooms on AOL and Gay.com can supply a virtually endless array of horny ready-to-fuck guys in most cities. One—or several—of them can be at your doorstep sporting nothing but a leather jock-strap and a cat-o'-nine-tails in 30 minutes flat. And there are other men-for-men Web sites that will tantalize you with pictures of anonymous, virtually fat-free gym bods and disembodied nine-inch dicks. These sites and services, which are strictly aimed at gay men looking for a quickie fuck, promise a smorgasbord of sexual options. The sales pitch: All you need to do is sign on, put your picture online with a short description of your preferred sexual positions, list your endowment in (exaggerated) inches, give a fake age if you're over 30 and a fake waist size if it's over 32, pepper your profile with the requisite acronyms (like VLG, s2r, HngNHot, etc.), and pay $9.95 a month. Supposedly you're then virtually guaranteed some ass or cock whenever you get the urge. That's the unwritten promise, anyhow.

Because the Internet is anonymous by its very nature, it has the dubious benefit of allowing users' true identities to remain hidden while they post any number of fantasy (or outdated) images on their Web site profiles. You must be mindful of the dangers of a condition known as Internet short-sightedness (IS). It's a condition wherein a computer user finds that all the blood drains from his head and goes to his dick—the hard dick he's holding in one hand while he's typing on his computer keyboard with the other hand.

The variety of options in an online buffet, and the willingness of so many gay men to jump at the option of no-strings-attached sex, has both benefits and drawbacks, and one of the biggest drawbacks is IS. The short-term result of IS: a reduction in one's ability to think clearly and to make rational decisions about sexual partners. This might cause one to extrapolate incorrectly from a set of profile data about a potential fuck. Does this mean guys lie online? Well, yes—and no.

Say you're horny. You're home on a Thursday night and your fuck buddy is not answering his phone. You're tired of your DVD porn, and you'd prefer the company of a real-life gentleman caller anyway. You laptop is just sitting there...waiting to be used as a hook-up tool. You sign on to *www.Men4SexWithHotMenWithBigDicksRightNow.com* as HungTop69—because you can't think of a profile name any more imaginative than that. You do a search for profiles in your geographic area, and one profile, belonging to VGLjockBttm, pops up and catches your eye. It reads: "6' 180#, blond hair, big dick, total bottom." The accompanying picture shows a buffed, headless torso.

An online chat along these lines takes place via IM:

HungTop69: Hey man, what's up?

VGLjockBttm: Nothing much. Horny. You?

HungTop69: Same. Nice profile. Where r u?

VGLjockBttm: Thanks. Near the mall on Main St. You?

HungTop69: Not far. I'm by the airport.

VGLjockBttm: Cool. What u looking 4?

HungTop69: Don't know. Love oral, looking to fuck. You?

VGLjockBttm: Looking to get plowed. Got a pic?

HungTop69: Sure, wanna swap? Face pic?

VGLjockBttm: Sorry, just have X-rated.

HungTop69: OK, let's trade.

[short delay while pictures are uploaded and e-mailed.]

VGLjockBttm: Nice cock. What u into?

HungTop69: Nothing too kinky. You traveling?

VGLjockBttm: I can be. Send address. [...] Got it. Can be there in 20 minutes.

Look familiar? Yes, it can be that quick and easy, assuming

that you meet someone online who is as eager for a quickie hookup as you are.

Bzzzzzapppppp! You've just triggered the Booty Call Disaster Alarm! If this had been an actual online hookup, you could've been in for some serious disappointment.

VGLjockBttm might be a perfectly sweet, attractive, sexually voracious guy, just like he claims to be online. He might be drug- and disease-free, he might share your tastes in porn, and he might like to cuddle (or not) just like you do (or don't) after the hot, animalistic sex you imagine the two of you will have. On the other hand—and you'd never know until he arrives on your doorstep—he may be a snaggletoothed troll with a drug problem, a lingering STD, and bad oral hygiene. You may never actually know what you've reeled in until you see him in the flesh, and you may never find out about the STD unless he's scrupulously truthful.

If you're after an online hookup, you really need to ask your potential partner some pretty specific questions, like the ones you'll find in the examples below. If he can't or won't answer them, then you should move on. There are other cyberfish in the cybersea. Questions you should always ask before hooking up with a Web crawler:

Do you have a face picture? If he says no, the guy is likely (a) closeted, (b) partnered, or (c) terrified of the prospect of a cyberencounter with someone he knows offline—like a coworker or a relative. Solution? There's no shame in putting your face picture in a traditional personals ad online ("traditional" sites don't usually have m4m in the URL). Putting a face picture online is a very common practice in the new millennium, so if you're worried about identifying yourself with a photo, then maybe you ought to reconsider your profile name or the dirty details of your personal description.

Do you have another photo? In the age of Photoshop, any digital image can be manipulated to enhance a guy's best features and to hide a multitude of sins. Your cyberslut buddy could easily be a full 20 years older than he claims to be. With a second photo, at least you'll be able to make comparisons to get a slightly better sense of the truth.

Are you partying? While this sounds like an innocent enough question, it actually lets you know that your online amour is operating his delicate machinery under the influence of drugs. If he is, he's statistically far less likely to practice safe sex. And anecdotally speaking, guys on drugs are lousy lays. Tweakers often can't get hard, and they often don't get off. A nice little side effect of crystal meth is obsessive masturbation. You can decide whether that's a plus. Oh, then add grinding teeth and endless chatter to a limp dick. Paints a pretty picture, don't it?

What's your HIV status? Regardless of whether you're positive or negative, it's your responsibility to be up front about your status and to ask about the status of your partner. While it's safest to assume that all your partners are HIV-positive and to have safe sex accordingly, it's foolish not to find out.

Do you practice safe sex? There are guys who actively choose not to practice safe sex, and there are no common denominators for how they look, act, dress, or what they're into in the sack. You should simply know what you're in for if you're ordering in. Remember: You have the right to demand safe sex. If your current cyberbuddy isn't interested in safe sex, the next one is just a click or two away.

After all of these questions, you may find that the guy who

ends up on your doorstep is a tall, gorgeous Greek god of a man, a vision of perfection with all 10 fingers and toes, a nine-inch dick, and muscles sculpted from granite. Or he may be four inches shorter and 10 hard years older than he claimed online. Or he may be a cracked-out psycho. A certain amount of flexibility is required when you order in, but a cracked-out psycho is rarely a menu item you should be willing to substitute for prime man meat.

If he's a loon, then having an exit strategy at the ready is essential. See the last section in this chapter for a psycho escape plan.

If he's not cuckoo but he's still not the chiseled Adonis he reported himself to be, he might still be kind of hot (if, for example, his photo was only five years old). Or he may be just passable (his photo was five years old, shot through cheesecloth while he was lying on his back, and digitally retouched). But since it's just a sex hookup—rather than something more intimate like a dinner date—you should reserve the option to bow out if he has misrepresented himself, without guilt or fuss on your part.

Alan, 35, a music label executive in Los Angeles, won't give a potential online date his address until after he has spoken on the phone with the person. "It's not a surefire way to weed out the weirdos, but it certainly helps," Alan reports. "Even if I've seen a picture, talking on the phone helps me get a much clearer mental picture of the guy than an online profile does. If he sounds like he's into stuff that creeps me out, or if he doesn't care whether I'm positive or negative, then I won't meet him."

Keeping some flexibility in mind, it's always good to establish one ground rule before meeting in the flesh: Make sure he's cool with a cordial in-person "hello" before the clothes come off. It's a chance for you to evaluate one another before stripping naked. Backing out when your pants are around your ankles is still your prerogative, but it's a little harder to do than when you're both dressed. If either of you catches a weird vibe or is turned off, you have the option to say goodbye without any bad feelings.

To help ensure that your online hookup experiences are good ones, here are a few pointers on making the most of your online profile.

• **_Describe yourself accurately._** Imagine what other guys might want to know about you before they e-mail or IM you. Include your age, interests, and build. Whatever else you choose to divulge, it's only fair to include those basic details. You'd want to know them too, right? Don't ever put "e-mail me to find out" when you're answering a profile prompt. Online cruisers will ignore it.

• **_Be specific._** So you like music and movies. Who doesn't? Offer specific examples of your tastes. Describing your interests in Slayer and _Night of the Living Dead_ or Kylie Minogue and Meg Ryan movies is far more explicit and effective. Your personality will start to take shape in someone else's mind much more clearly, and he'll more likely be intrigued and want to find out more. You've offered the ingredients for a good online conversation, and your Mr. Right Now will ping you much more quickly.

• **_Don't be the dope who spells "discreet" the wrong way._** (Yes, there are two ways: _discrete_ means separate or distinct, while _discreet_ means tactful or prudent.) This isn't an essay test, but online readers will take your profile much more seriously if they think you can capitalize, use proper grammar, and spell correctly. Write your profile, then go over it before you post it (maybe even ask a friend to read it) to check for errors.

• *Show your humor.* Heaven knows there are plenty of guys online without a sense of humor. Let the world know you're not one of them by adding a touch of wit to your profile. Include a funny quote from your favorite movie (*Steel Magnolias*: "All gay men have track lightin'. And all gay men are named Mark, Rick, or Steve."), or a song lyric that you especially like, or anything by Oscar Wilde ("A little sincerity is a dangerous thing, and a great deal of it is absolutely fatal."). It should reflect you, or at least the guy you want to be.

While you're at it:

• *Do not lie.* If you lie about your age, weight, build, or dick size, he'll know when he shows up on your doorstep (or soon thereafter). You don't want to be caught in a lie.

• *Do not write a whole essay, or your life story, or your plans for overthrowing the government.* Keep that no-margins, tiny-scripted manifesto in your loose-leaf binder for your own personal use. Or do what all other netizens of the 21st century feel the need to do: Keep a blog for all that useless shit. Your personal profile should be relatively short and sweet.

• *Don't include your address.* Don't include your phone number—even if it's spelled out, like "two-one-two-five-five-five..." etc. You may have worked your way around the Internet service provider's phone-number detector bot, but you will look totally desperate. Serial killers have computers too. You never know who might be reading your profile or ad, and no one wants to hook up with someone who will hook up with anyone.

What to Do When He Has Very Small Equipment

I would never insist that size doesn't matter. Clearly it matters to plenty of people, or the question wouldn't even come up. If it truly didn't matter, certain spammers and "herbal enhancement" merchants would all go broke. But our insecurities about our equipment (all men, gay and straight) keep them in business.

There's a vast population of size queens and huge-cock worshippers out there. The worlds of porn and the Internet have conspired to satisfy those who pray at the altar of the colossal cock, and they've simultaneously made many of us insecure when it comes to the size of our own equipment.

Using standards derived from gay porn, combined with the impression you'll get from cruising online, you might reasonably guess that average endowment is roughly eight inches. Medical science has a slightly different take on the size of the average dick. The average dick, fully erect, is somewhere between five and six inches. That's still plenty of dick, by the way. Some dicks are smaller than average too. While size matters to many—specifically the aforementioned size queens and other big-dick worshippers—it doesn't matter that much to everyone. While your new partner might not be hung like a horse, smaller dicks can still be plenty of fun.

"Big-dicked guys sometimes don't get hard all the way," says Andrew, 42, a landscape architect in Dallas, explaining his fondness for guys with small cocks. He has even joined an online club where guys with similar interests can swap pictures and meet. In fact, there are dozens of such Web sites and online groups available for interested men.

Even though many men assume that having a big dick makes someone a top, that's not necessarily the case. Men with small endowments aren't always bottoms, either. And there's just no correlation between masculinity and the size of your bulge.

If you're open to the possibilities, you'll discover that there are advantages to getting it on with a smaller-hung guy: it's easier to suck him off because you can fit more of him into your mouth, and it can make it easier for him to fuck you. Some guys prefer partners with smaller dicks because they imagine that they're at some kind of sexual advantage— the smaller-dicked guy is just drooling to get at the bigger-dicked guy's cock. Todd, 21, a student in New Orleans, loves playing with guys who are less endowed that he is. "I get a charge out of being the bigger one. I'm not always the top, but I'm not exactly a great bottom yet, so playing with a guy with a smaller cock makes it easier for me to bottom."

Some anal sex positions are ideally suited for a top guy wielding a Vienna sausage rather than a kielbasa. The **high heels** position gives the top the maximum amount of penetration. (Because the bottom guy is on his back with his legs spread, the angle allows for deep penetration.) Guys who can't normally bottom this way can handle the position just fine when taking a smaller sausage. The classic **doggie style** allows for this kind of deep penetration as well.

Whether it's big or small, his package size is a result of heredity and genetics—and nothing else. As for schemes designed to plump up the pecker? Skip 'em. The herbal enhancements have been proven to be snake oil. Penis pumps will only plump you up temporarily; there are no long-term benefits, and there are some serious risks involved with pumps. As for dick-enhancing surgery, the jury is still out—the most common technique involves cutting the suspensory ligaments so that your dick simply hangs lower. It's not any longer, and you won't be able to make it jump when it's erect by flexing your pelvic muscles. Love your love-wand—and his—just as it is.

What to Do When You're Both Bottoms

There's something to be said for the virtue of versatility. The most important aspect of being versatile is that you can hang out in the humpy hammock with whomever you like. If you're decidedly a bottom and your hookup for the evening is too (a not uncommon occurrence), you've got a few options. Your first option is to do some of the other stuff we gay boys love to do—like oral sex, rimming, *frottage,* masturbation, or a ***Princeton belly rub,*** for example. (These are also great methods of man-lovin' for the many guys who never take it up the poop chute and still have totally fulfilling sex lives.)

You can give the nonpenetrative method a shot, or you can dust off that double-headed dildo and take turns using it on one another—or, better yet, use it simultaneously. Toys like dildos, anal beads, and vibrators are great for one-at-a-time sex: you use it on him, and then he uses it on you. (Be sure to put a clean condom on that cattle prod when you swap out.) Just because you're not a top doesn't mean that you can't have fun playing with his ass.

You can try topping, of course. If you'd like to top your partner but you have trouble staying hard with a condom on, try a cock ring for added firmness, or strap on a strap-on. What's not to like? It's dick-shaped, it's hard, and it's kinky. Strap-ons: They're not just for lesbians!

Another option is to bring in a top to fuck you both. While this isn't a great idea for first dates or a romantic weekend, if you're just meeting a guy for the first time and you both know your mission is just to get off, then what difference would it make to turn your pas de deux into a ménage à trois? Call a fuck buddy or cruise the bars together. Even if you don't end up with a third, the sexual excitement of looking for one with a fellow bottom could kick your mojo into high gear.

What to Do When You're Both Tops

Some people would contend that this is an exceedingly rare occurrence (most of those people live in Los Angeles). You may have a more difficult time convincing your total-top fuck buddy to switch roles than you'll have convincing a bottom guy. In the event your sword fight turns into a standoff and no one is willing to bend over for the cause, how are you to proceed? You can try the oral stuff—especially sixty-nine. Two tops sucking each other off simultaneously can be super fun. Like the bottom guys above, you can look for a third—this time you'll be looking for someone to provide the desired orifice. The prospect of getting fucked by two horny top guys is something some power bottoms simply can't pass up.

Another option is to engage in a little *interfemoral intercourse,* the common practice of the ancient Greeks. This activity replicates the body positions and sensations of penetrative sex, but no one actually gets penetrated, which makes it cool for two tops and also makes it a very low-risk sexual activity.

Picture it: George B. and Dick C. are two closeted guys who cruise each other in a seedy bar while their wives are off at a Junior League meeting. George takes Dick back to his double-wide trailer—the one he keeps for his illicit homosexual affairs—and gets Dick tipsy and naked. After chowing down on each other's butts for a good long while, George lubes up his cock and puts Dick facedown on the bed. He gets Dick to hold his legs together and slides his cock in between Dick's ass cheeks, though not into his butt hole. After a while Dick turns over and they lie face-to-face, with each one sliding his dick between the other guy's thighs. Dick comes first, then tells George when it's OK for him to come. That, my friends, is how two tight-asses can fuck each other without either of them having to say he took it up the ass.

What to Do When He Thinks You're Boyfriends After One Night

There's a big difference between sweet and psycho. *Sweet* is when you met a guy at the linens store at the mall and invite him out for dinner, drinks, and a roll in the hay on your new Egyptian cotton sheets. And he calls you the next day to say how much fun it was and to see if you want to do it again. *Psycho* is when the guy who blew you in the mall bathroom calls you every 15 minutes for a week afterward until you have to change your mobile number. Somewhere in between is a guy who was a fun fuck but who has decided that your tryst was more than a one-time thing and he thinks you're boyfriends now.

Say you don't want a boyfriend, or you're not interested in *him* as a boyfriend. Should you let him down easy or just be blunt? Should you drop casual hints or crush him like a bug? Remember that what comes around goes around. You need to be honest with him, and firm. You don't want to leave any gray area that he might misinterpret as interest on your part—he'll only end up resenting you when you don't come through.

The best and fastest way to be clear with him is to say, "I'm sorry if you misinterpreted our meeting. I had a terrific time, but it was only a one-time thing. I'm not in the market for a boyfriend right now." The worst thing you can do is to invite him over for a second round. A lovelorn guy will very likely misinterpret a second naked game of Twister as romantic interest. You can't meet him for coffee, or go to the movies with him, or have lengthy discussions about why he's not the guy for you, and you certainly can't fuck around with him again. It's cruel.

If he was a friend before you jumped into bed, then you're in trouble. Extricating yourself from that sticky situation will require a lot of patience and finesse.

What to Do When You Did it With a Good Friend

It can happen to any of us. Normally, he's your "wingman," to employ a hetero, *Top Gun*-esque term. He's the friend who loudly announces to the entire bar that your car is being towed, so you can make a quick getaway from the grabby barfly who's trying to get into your pants. He's the buddy who scrapes you off the bathroom floor when the many pitchers of margaritas you consumed begin to exact their sloppy revenge.

He's also the guy who gets drunk with you, increasing the chance that you'll end up almost passed out on the floor in his bedroom together, where your legs touching ever so slightly can quickly turn into a pornorific, full-fledged fuckfest.

That's when you did it.

Maybe you shouldn't have done it. He's really *just* a friend. Not only have you seen his questionable pickup techniques on other guys too many times to consider him alluring, but also he's important to you as a friend and you don't want to crush his ego by hinting that you don't find him attractive enough to fuck when you're sober. It's a delicate balance, and you've splooged all over it.

True, plenty of gay men meet their mates this way. The reverse is true too: Many gay men make friends by fucking around with someone only to find that they're better suited as a buddy than a boyfriend. But, in the interest of preserving your friendship with your wingman, you'll want to ease your way out of the sexual situation.

Before you can start acting awkward around one another at your weekly brunch with other friends, just start off by saying how weird it was that you two hooked up. Not weird-icky, but weird-funny. If he agrees, then you're home free and the chance that either of you will mention it to your brunch mates is slim.

Bottom line: Try not to sleep with your friends. Unless you're part of a post-hippie free-love collective, the politics surrounding sex with friends is just too complicated.

What To Do When He's an Absolute Psycho

There's a fine line between guys who are eccentric in a way that's strangely alluring and guys who have totally lost their shit. The challenge is to suss out the psycho before he pole-vaults over that fine line and into your life. It doesn't matter how you've come to know him. He could be the online trick who has a collection of python moltings next to the bed, or he could be the guy who seemed nice enough at dinner but got too rough (like, bruising you) when you started getting frisky together. Get up, get dressed, get out, and don't look back.

If you meet an online date for anything especially kinky, it might not be a bad idea to leave word with a friend about your plans—not the specifics, just the location and how long you'll be away. An hour? A weekend? Until the feeling returns to your nipples? Especially if your tryst involves kinkiness that requires expert skill (BDSM, fisting, electricity play), then make sure you're playing with someone who has been referred to you or whom you've met through friends. But if you're playing with a stranger, or if you aren't sure whether your kinkmate is just interested in a little light spanking or wants to mummify you, then you might make a little show of calling a friend when you arrive at your kinkmaster's place. Just so he gets that other people know where you are.

If you suddenly become unsettled in your setting, if you feel as though you could possibly be cornered or jumped, or if you feel that your safety is being threatened in any way, then have an escape route planned.

Boyd, 35, a computer sales representative in Tulsa, Oklahoma, recalls a close encounter of the cuckoo kind with a guy he'd met on a phone sex line: "We seemed to be into each other and into the same stuff sexually, so he invited me over. I went to his place and he kept trying to pressure me into bottoming for him—which isn't something I do with anyone except a long-term boyfriend. I said no and we continued making out. This guy was big and he kept getting more and more forceful, and then he started lunging at me and grabbing really roughly at my ass. He might have been high or just nuts. I started to get up and leave and he pushed me back down. Rather than get worked up, I just lay back and said, 'OK, just give me a minute' and started to scratch at my crotch. He looked confused, so I said, 'It only flares up every once in a while,' and continued scratching. He assumed I had herpes or crabs or something, and faster than you can say 'free clinic' he was showing me out."

The important thing is to make sure you're thinking with your head—rather than your groin. The best way to get out of a really dangerous situation is not to get into it in the first place, so make sure you do a gut-check periodically to see whether your Spidey sense is going off. If he's not kosher, then make your exit before your clothes come off. I guarantee he won't be your last sexual encounter. And when all else fails, you can always make a date with your hand, bucko.

7 THE MORNING AFTER

You two (or three or four) had a great, sweaty, lusty time. Now what are you going to do? Negotiating the gray areas in relationships—even purely sexual relationships—takes a little care and understanding. Even confirmed bachelor studs have to understand how to navigate the sexual seas with their tricks. One must learn the finer points of different kinds of relationships so as not to send mixed signals. Getting this wrong might mean that you—whether deservedly or not—develop a reputation as a player (never a good thing) and the news will get around quickly; your status as a lout will get around even faster. And do you really want to have to hop on a plane to a distant city just to boff guys who haven't heard about your bad rep before?

in the Market for a Fuck Buddy

Sometimes you're only in the mood for a one-time fling with the hot guy you met at the grocery store. Other times the sex is so sweaty and fun that you have to have him again—but you're not really interested in dating. He shops nearby, so he probably lives nearby, right?

Now you're faced with a decision. Do you leave the one experience alone, writing about your night of passion in your journal and making a mental note of the love bites on your ass and the rug burns on your knees? Or do you get his number before he takes off and ask if he wants a rematch?

If you picked the latter, you're in the market for a fuck buddy (FB). A fuck buddy is that guy you know who comes over with some regularity—or you go to his place—and you fuck each other's brains out. That's it. You're not dating. You're just fucking. Hence the name.

Why have a fuck buddy? The appeal can involve having sex with someone with whom you share almost nothing in common. For example, you might never consider dating a Republican, but if he's hot you might just want to *hate-fuck* him twice a month. Not that you need to be a naughty boy (you bought this book, so you're already qualified), but there is something thrillingly transgressive about meeting up with someone for sex—with no niceties involved at all.

This arrangement works out really well for guys who can't or won't get involved in a romantic relationship. It's an association that occurs when your libidos are aligned. It's safer than cruising parks and public toilets for action. You never have to worry about dating. There are no restaurants, no little gifts just because, no dressing up in your newest togs for him, no commitments, no going with him to his cousin Sally's son's bar mitzvah, no arguments, no emotion.

Usually.

Making FB arrangements sounds easy enough: You cruised a hot man, you liked the hot sex, and you made plans to do it again in a week or two. But our hearts and groins are not always in perfect agreement with one another. Sometimes your FB can turn into a crush, or it can morph into dating—without your even realizing it. How do you know if the guy you're having sex with is your FB? Answer these questions to find out:

1. Do you know his last name?
2. Do you know his "legit" e-mail address? ("Legit" address-es do not include references to his dick size or a sexual position, nor do they include the words *jock, stud,* or *boi.*)
3. Do you know what he does for a living?
4. Has he ever introduced you to his roommates or friends—by your real name?
5. Have you ever intentionally met up with him anywhere other than your place or his, or for a purpose other than sex?

If you answered no to most of these questions, chances are he's probably your FB. Either that or you're a total troglodyte who ought to learn your boyfriend's last name and take him out once in a while.

If you like your relationship as it is and you're serious about maintaining the sex-only status of your rendezvous, you have a few options. The first and most direct option is to tell him, "Hey man, I'd be totally into us being fuck buddies, but I'm not really into dating anyone. You cool with that? What do you say to us getting our freak on again?" You can also say it without the phrase, "getting our freak on," if you prefer. If he agrees to your offer, you've essentially made a pact that whatever happens between you is all in the name of getting off and that no one's feelings are going to get hurt.

You're not free and clear for a lifetime of emotion-free sex just yet. Your FB relationship requires maintenance too. By learning and honoring the unspoken code of the FB you will be able to keep the sex/romance line from blurring. Make sure you are clear with your FB that your encounters are sex dates—not romantic ones—by keeping the duration of your meetings to the time it takes to get undressed, get off, shower, and get dressed again. Avoid postcoital cuddling after you've gotten your breath back. Go ahead and offer him a drink, but not a meal. Don't linger too long after sex, and don't agree to do something friendly, like see a movie together or get a cup of coffee.

Alan met his fuck buddy on a blind date. They were not meant to be lovers, it seems, just FBs. "My friend Emma set me up with her neighbor Russ, and I picked him up at his apartment to go to dinner. I hated the way he'd decorated his place. It was like Martha Stewart vomited up pale yellow plaids and shitted chenille all over the place. It was a fiesta of right angles. He had a mean cat—and it had a first and a last name. I hated everything he ordered at dinner and he hated everything I ordered. He had no interest in politics and no knowledge of the world beyond Restoration Hardware. It was a disaster, and the feeling was mutual. But he had these perfect full lips, thick hair, and an ass so pert you could rest your drink on it. So when I dropped him off, I sort of invited myself in.

"It didn't take much to become fuck buddies. I'd e-mail him on the weekends, and if he wasn't shopping, he'd come over and we'd take turns fucking each other. We never talked much, which was just fine by me. I never saw him out and about, and our circles of friends didn't overlap, except for Emma. Neither of us told Emma we were fucking. As far as she knew, the first date was the last. When it was over, it was over. There was no drama. I'd love to get him into bed once more, but I'd never have dinner with him again."

If you do start to develop a crush on your FB, let him know right away that you'd like to talk about dating. Despite the old adage, FBs of the kind described by Alan and Russ—total polar opposites—tend not to get involved in real life, just in Nora Ephron movies (and one of these men would have to be Meg Ryan). Still, it is possible to harbor secret feelings or to start wondering what your FB is up to when he doesn't have his dick down your throat. So you better talk about your feelings with him. It's better to know immediately if he feels the same way you do. Relationships can and do start out this way, but if you're not both on the same page, then no matter how hot the sex was, you've got to end the meetings. To continue to have sex, once one of you is emotionally involved and the other isn't, can cause hurt feelings or heartbreak.

Some guys know they have a tendency to fall for men they're having sex with, so they limit their nonromantic encounters to once or twice with a guy, then they move on. Do what's right for you, always remembering to play safe, and be honest with your partners about your intentions. A little communication and mutual understanding can help you develop a superhot no-strings arrangement.

The Booty Call

When *The Washington Post* is writing about it and Vivica A. Fox is starring in movies about it, the booty call can hardly be considered an underground phenomenon. The booty call, for the uninitiated (and just where have you been?), is a phone call for the purpose of sex. The call is typically made late at night, involves very little conversation, and is often between people who would have little to do with one another if they weren't fucking, or about to fuck.

How is this different from cruising online or in a bar or on a phone-sex line for a one-nighter? For starters, since it's a person-to-person call, you need to know the phone number of the person whose bumper you want to pull up to. Because the pretext is sex without pretense (no flirt, no cruise), the BC requires an acknowledged FB relationship—or the guy you're calling will just assume you're a drunk asshole when he hears you slur, "So what are you up to right now?" at 2:30 A.M.

A booty call differs from a phone-sex line or online hookup in a few other ways. Take a look at these comparisons to determine which approach is best for you.

Prime time

Booty Call: Friday or Saturday night from midnight to 4 A.M. Do not call before 9 P.M.

Online Hookup: Evenings and weekends, anytime—just like your cell phone plan.

Phone-Sex Hookup: Evenings and weekends.

How will being drunk affect your hookup?

Booty Call: DWI (dialing while intoxicated) may yield the wrong number. Try not to drunk-dial your mom for sex.

Online Hookup: TWI (typing while intoxicated) can be difficult and tedious.

Phone-Sex Hookup: UATTKWI (using a touch-tone keypad while intoxicated), you may have trouble navigating the touch-tone menu.

Prior introductions

Booty Call: Required. You need to know your intended sex partner well enough to invite him over for sex.

Online Hookup: Not necessary. Let your online profile be your introduction.

Phone-Sex Hookup: Not necessary.

Chitchat factor

Booty Call: Not required, unless this is your first booty call with your intended. You don't have shit to discuss.

Online Hookup: Occasionally required. Beware endless instant messaging.

Phone-Sex Hookup: Not required. Heavy breathing and/or phone sex does not count as chitchat.

Anonymity factor

Booty Call: Impossible to be anonymous, unless you misdial a willing stranger.

Online Hookup: Possible to be anonymous, unless you trade photos prior to meeting in real time.

Phone-Sex Hookup: Possible to be anonymous, because you cannot see the other callers on the line.

How not to appear desperate

Booty Call: It's not desperate if you and your FB have an understanding about hookups for sex.

Online Hookup: You're not desperate until you've been typing with your pants off for an hour.

Phone-Sex Hookup: Always desperate, but so are all the other guys on the line, so embrace the desperation.

Suave come-ons

Booty Call: "Hey, want to come over?"
Online Hookup: "Trade pictures?"
Phone-Sex Hookup: "What are you wearing?"

Should he stay over?

Booty Call: Only if it was really good and you want morning sex.
Online Hookup: Never.
Phone-Sex Hookup: Never.

is dirty talk allowed prior to meeting in the flesh?

Booty Call: Yes.

Online Hookup: Yes. Sometimes a little cybersex foreplay is also required.

Phone-Sex Hookup: Hell, yes. It's a requirement.

Hindsight is 20/20

It's possible to cross the line with an FB, an online hookup, or a phone-sex line date (collectively called "tricks" below). By doing something indicative of a more intimate or personal relationship, you may irreparably damage your rather tenuous sex-only relationship. If either of you does something to cross the line, it's often an indication that one of you hasn't fully compartmentalized his feelings about sex (separating sex from the idea of a romantic relationship) or that one of you would actually prefer to be dating—as opposed to fucking around. (And by the way, if you decide you're actually looking for someone to date, don't go looking for tricks hoping they'll change into dates. Though it can happen, it usually doesn't.)

You've crossed the line...

• ...if you end up cooking him breakfast in the morning. Now you're dating. Or worse: He's a trick that you have to cook for.

• ...if you feel like you had to make an excuse—any excuse— to leave or get your trick to leave after you've come and cleaned up. Tricks with an FB understanding don't require excuses.

• ...if you offer to pick him up or drop him off before or after sex. All tricks should provide their own transportation.

• ...if he suggests that you go without condoms. He should be tossed out immediately.

• ...if he asks you over to watch a movie (and he doesn't mean *I Dream of Weenie* or *Splendor in the Ass*). That's a date.

• ...if you're meeting a trick before or after the rendezvous for drinks or dinner. Now you're dating.

• ...if you've ever thought of your trysts as "lovemaking," or your trick as a "lover." Probably from watching too many Italian movies.

• ...if you ever compare each other to former lovers. Your past is of no concern to him, and his is none of your business.

• ...if you've made hook-up plans more than a few hours in advance. That's dating. Exceptions include sex dates made in advance when you're traveling.

• ...if you've ever mailed anything to him, like a holiday card or birthday greeting—even a sleazy one. You shouldn't be thinking about him when he's not naked; that's a sign that you wish you were dating.

But don't worry...

• ...if he calls you the wrong name during sex. It's cool. You haven't gone too far. You're merely each other's means of getting off, so you're not allowed to take this personally.

• ...if he asks you if he can bring along a third. That's cool. Double your pleasure, double your fun.

SLEEPING-AROUND ETIQUETTE

8

You can be a stud without lying, cheating, stealing, or hurting anyone, if you do it properly. This chapter is all about how not to be rude when you're being a naughty boy.

Don't Hurt His Feelings

If you're just looking for a hookup rather than a relationship, you have to be up front with your new fuck friends about this fact, or they may mistake your intentions and wind up with hurt feelings.

While it's true that many a lovely LTR has blossomed from a sweaty one-night stand, it's not really all that common. More often than not, two guys meet, do it, and go their separate ways. But men who are looking for love—and engaging in one-nighters—often have the superhuman ability to hear things that are not said ("I know we're strangers and we just fucked, but I really want to date you") and see things that didn't happen ("he gave me a look that said, *I want you to stalk me!*"). Yes, even when the hormone-soaked occasion of your first meeting seems fleeting and impersonal, some guys will mis-understand your sex-only approach. Not all guys have learned to separate love from sex, so it's important not to confuse a sex buddy by leading him on.

How do you avoid hurting a sex buddy's feelings? For starters—especially when you're fucking—don't tell him that you love him. Don't tell him you could really use a boyfriend like him. Don't whisper sweet nothings, don't flatter him too much, and don't promise to call him to hang out when all you want from him is some ass.

If your new FB doesn't want to be just a FB, he's entitled to ask you for more. Since you're now having "the talk" (see below), you in turn are entitled to tell him what you want, and if your desires and wishes don't match, then you're both enti-tled to seek out other people whose interests match your own. You're *not* entitled to lie to him, to be romantic for the pur-pose of seducing him into bed, or to simply not tell him the sordid truth (that you just want sex), hoping he'll figure it out on his own.

Be Prepared for "The Talk"

Even if they're fine with your sex-only understanding, guys you're fucking around with might eventually want to discuss "where things are going." This conversation, in relationship vernacular, is called "the talk," and it never starts out well. If you and your FB are of like minds and you both want to con-tinue in your no-strings-attached relationship—or if you both like each other on a more intimate level and you want to progress to dating, with all its attendant perks and obligations to one another—then fantastic! "The talk" went well. In any case, you have to be prepared to have the talk to determine if you are on the same page and either to embark on a relationship with your former sex-only buddy or to cut off your FB relationship so no one gets hurt.

To Spend or Not to Spend the Night. That is the Question

You are better off establishing your thoughts on the sleepover topic before either of you falls into a postcoital snooze. Some guys just assume that a hearty game of slap and tickle also includes a sleepover at your place. Sometimes you just want the slapping with none of the spooning. If you suspect that your *paramour du jour* is going to want to nap after the nookie, then it's best to lay down the ground rules (without sounding like you're laying down ground rules) before he arrives on your doorstep.

If you ordered out via a phone-sex line (how '90s!) or the Internet, your playdate should not expect to be offered a pillow after your meeting of the minds, so no explanation will be required when you each towel off and you show him the door. Such a meeting is often just:

- casual greeting
- clothes come off
- action begins
- action ends
- visitor gets dressed
- visitor goes home

You might, however, ask your man of the minute if he'd like to shower off before hitting the road. Plus, maybe he'll invite you into the shower with him for round two before he goes home. Just because he's a trick and he's not sleeping over doesn't mean you can be impolite.

If, however, your randy rendezvous is a first-time hookup with a legitimate date—or someone you brought home from a party, club, or bar (or you know each other's last names)—then a simple "I've got an early appointment in the morning, so I can't invite you to stay the night" will suffice nicely. The gentlemanly thing to do would be to make sure he has transportation home or at least call him a cab—unless you and your trick haven't even traded first names, in which case he's on his own to find his way home.

Since this is a matter of politeness and respect, you should expect the same from him. If he invites you to his place and you'd rather not spend the night, don't assume you've got an invitation. Just lace up your sneakers and head out. If he asks, "Hey! Where are you going?" then consider that an invitation to stay and spoon.

All things considered, it's never appropriate to ring a fireman's bell and yell, "Two A.M.! Closing time! You don't have to go home, but you can't stay here!" after he ejaculates.

Don't Just Call Him When You're Drunk

Booze and boys mix pretty damn well most of the time. A little alcohol will boost your confidence. It will break the ice between strangers. It will lower your inhibition levels and give you that little bit of liquid courage you need to say hi to Mr. Tall, Dark, and Hunky. It will make you a better dancer! It will turn you into the most important person in the room! Um, right. OK, so a little liquor is good, and too much is *too much.*

You might think you're drop-dead sexy when the apple martinis are stacked up inside you. But your FB, boyfriend, ménage à trois buddy, or other sex-on-call friend on the other end of the phone line may think that your slurry, "Oh baby, I need your lovin' " is a less than enticing offer. One or two calls is forgivable—on your birthday only—but if you're routinely high or drunk when you're calling him for sex, he'll rightly assume that you either have a drinking problem or you don't think highly enough of him to call when you're sober. This isn't about relationships. This is about respect.

Polite Sex in Public Places

Hot sex can make you lose track of your surroundings. When your pants are down and your stiff dick is in someone's warm, wet mouth, it's entirely possible to forget that before you lost track of the real world, you were actually standing in an alley or jammed into your car in a parking lot. Or perhaps you were fumbling in the shrubs in a public park or squashed between boxes of toner in a supply closet in your office.

When you're having sex in public you must realize that your actions are most likely illegal (outdoor sex is not legal in any public place in the country). If you get caught—or almost caught—doing the deed, you've got to button up and fly right as quickly as possible. Stand, don't recline. Pull clothes only partially off or just pull them aside so you can quickly don your gay apparel if need be. If you're in an alleyway and disturb anyone who claims the alley as his home, give him a couple of bucks and find a new spot pronto.

Even getting nude in public is super risky. Unless you're at a nude beach, keep Mr. Bo and the Jangles in your Speedo. Your honey might like a peek at your poker, but if you're streaking or peeking in any location where there are children who might catch a glimpse, you'll have the morality police on your ass right quick.

Porn

Who doesn't love porn? Well, truth be told, it's not a universally loved art form, so if you're inviting a buddy over for some boisterous butt burgling, ask if he's into porn before popping *Field of Creams* into the DVD player. Setting a sex mood is vital, but it doesn't always include a fast-forward function for all guys. As for your magazine and DVD collection, keeping it out of plain sight in your apartment or house is a good idea. It's only polite not to inflict your triple-X tastes on the people who might pop in for nonsexual reasons.

Smoke, Pills, Sex, and Thrills

Drugs of all kinds are the subjects of many urban legends. You may have heard how amazing it is to have sex on ecstasy or suck cock on coke or how a bump or a line will send you into orbit.

Setting all the lore aside for a minute, here is the lowdown on what certain chemicals will do to your sex play, your inhibitions, and your judgment. All drugs can lower your inhibitions and many of them can have lasting effects on your libido, your mental health, and your ability to make decisions about safe sex. Here's a tip: If you're going to do drugs, make the safe-sex part of your encounter as easy as possible. Make sure you've got condoms and lube handy so that whatever troubles you may have (getting it up, aiming, concentrating for more than 10 seconds at a time), safe sex won't be one of them.

Cocaine: Coke is a stimulant and in small doses it can amp up your sexual desire and erectile function. In larger doses, it will make you a chattering, self-important ass, and it might make getting it up and getting off more difficult. It will impair your judgment, and you can get hooked on it.

LSD and magic mushrooms: They produce mild to wild hallucinations, and some people experience increased arousal. But the nature of the high varies dramatically, and many people get turned off and experience a lack of physical sensation. You can expect time warps and impaired judgment—plus, hallucinating a lizard tail on your FB is only arousing for a select few lizard fetishists.

Speed (amphetamines): The high may make you feel aroused, but ironically, it makes it harder for users to achieve an erection or orgasm. One variety in particular, crystal meth, makes users more susceptible to HIV infection and other STDs. It will greatly impair your judgment, and you can get hooked on crystal and other varieties of speed. Because amphetamines simultaneously make you more aroused and less likely to get hard and pop off, users can become chronic masturbators while they're high. Expect lots of penile chafing, gnashing of teeth, and voices in your head (but the voices will tell you you're much less tragic than you appear to be to others). Pretty!

Marijuana: Users experience lowered inhibitions and occasionally some touchy-feely enhancements of sensory perception, although other users can become withdrawn and less social. Weed will impair your judgment. Music might sound better, but you may find your concentration drifting, and you'll definitely get cotton mouth (bad for oral sex).

Ecstasy: Users get all warm, fuzzy, and blissful, and get way into touching each other. Getting hard and getting off can be much more difficult for some folks, but they'll still want to sit and stroke your hair for, like, six hours and say "wow" a lot. Users often forget to practice safe sex. Compound forgetfulness with the ecstatic (hence the name) sense of affection for everyone within make-out distance, and you might end up having risky sex with people you'd never touch with a 10-foot pole if you were sober. Plus, it saps your happy brain chemical serotonin, so you turn into a mopey bitch for a few days after coming down.

Heroin: This drug, in a class called opiates, has a painkilling effect. The experience is one of detachment, so it's not exactly ideal for sex. Repeated use can lead to impotence, reduced libido, and difficulty achieving orgasm. It will totally impair your judgment and you can get your hollow-eyed, jaundiced self hooked on the stuff. Track marks aren't so hot, either.

Poppers: Sniffing poppers creates a brief, intense head rush and a state of muscle relaxation. Users describe the feeling as a powerful, passionate disembodiment, like "being part of the sex." Side effects include a reduction in blood pressure, chronic sinus problems, and wicked headaches. Using poppers with Viagra, a drug that also reduces blood pressure, can be a fatal mix: Your heart might relax so much it will just stop. No one needs you to be *that* relaxed.

GHB: Gamma hydroxybutyrate is an odorless, colorless liquid sedative. It can cause dizziness, confusion, and loss of consciousness—and those are its selling points. It's super easy to overdose with, and it's a common date rape drug. The less appealing side affects include loss of memory, nausea, insomnia, tremors, and death.

Ketamine: Sometimes called Special K, Vitamin K, or Cat Valiums, it's most commonly used by veterinarians on large animals—and by non-veterinarians as a recreational intoxicant. It's most often snorted in small doses ("bumps") to create a dreamy, dissociative state—sort of like tripping, being stoned, and tits-up drunk all at once. Ketamine use can induce a "k-hole," a paranoid, agitated, and confused state (similar to what you might expect from prolonged viewing of the Home Shopping Network). It's potentially deadly when used with other depressants, and it can cause severe dehydration, especially if you're using it in a hot, sweaty dance club. The pain-numbing effect of this and many other drugs also means that, during sex, you might not feel tiny cuts and tears on your dick or in your ass. These cuts and tears can increase your susceptibility to HIV and STD transmission. All drugs can also have an adverse effects if you take them in combination with over-the-counter or prescription drugs.

Consider this too: Less can be more. Drugs that boost your sensory perception—like ecstasy, GHB, and ketamine—are most effective at low doses. Too much and you lose the pleasurable effect. And too much alcohol? It might get your engine started, but it will leave your body poorly prepared for action.

NONMONOGAMY AND COMING OUT OF A RELATIONSHIP

9

Plenty of guys meet the loves of their lives while participating in a little *cottaging*. Plenty of guys prefer to be single, and plenty of other guys wish they could get legally married and live the rest of their lives in wedded bliss with their partners. I won't get into a lengthy discussion about the merits of marriage—even when it's clear that if some people in the United States have the choice to get married, then all Americans should have the choice. Married or not, coupled or not, monogamy isn't for everyone, and not everyone believes you have to be sexually monogamous to be in a committed relationship.

In this chapter I describe some of the many permutations that gay relationships can take, what works for some couples who decide not to limit themselves to one sexual partner, and some of the common denominators for successful nonmonogamous relationships. I'll also take a look at tactics for guys who are interested in getting back into dating after having come out of long-term, monogamous relationships.

Does Monogamy Work?

Yes, my dear reader, monogamy can and does work for many gay men. You can tell Pat Robertson and the Christian Coalition and the Moral Majority to shut the fuck up when they proclaim that because you're gay, you are single-handedly destroying the nuclear family. (Angry, repressed heterosexuals are managing that little project just fine on their own.) Furthermore, don't let anyone tell you that you don't know the meaning of monogamy or a committed relationship, or that you deserve anything less—if that's what you want in your life. You can be as *Ozzie and Harriet* as you damn well please. And the naysayers can blow you.

There are gay men all across this country who are paired off and happily settled down in their suburban homes with white picket fences, vegetable gardens, and sensible sedans. There are monogamous, taxpaying, law-abiding homos in high-rise apartment buildings and in double-wide trailers. Being gay doesn't mean that monogamy is intrinsically less worthwhile for you than it is to anyone else. The beauty is that you get to decide! You can decide whether or not you want a monogamous relationship. No one is twisting your arm to get married, and no one is shoving you toward gay key parties. If you and your partner are committed to each other, practice monogamy, and have similar views about monogamy, then you too can be monogamous! Just like the heteros!

Monogamy isn't easy for anyone, though. Gay couples face the same difficulties that hetero couples and lesbians face when it comes to monogamy. We stray, we think other people are sexually appealing, we have trouble with fidelity—but we haven't cornered the market on these problems. We have these problems because we're *human,* not because we're gay.

So how do you get into a monogamous relationship, especially if you haven't been in one in the past? The kind of trust that monogamy and fidelity require grows gradually between two people. You have to be honest with your partner about the good stuff—like your desire to be committed—and about the bad stuff—like your fear of being involved in a committed relationship. You must get to know your partner well enough to be able to trust him. Your partner must feel the way you do about monogamy, or at least he has to care enough about you to be willing to consider a committed relationship and to discuss the terms of that with you. And you must feel that you're worth the effort: If you don't feel that you're worth his giving up sex with others, then why should *he* think you're worth it?

Open Relationships: Jason and Joseph

Jason, 31, and Joseph, 38, met through a mutual friend at Joseph's company holiday party. Their affair started quickly, and they quickly became boyfriends. That was five years ago.

"We were very up-front with each other right away," says Jason, "about the fact that neither of us thought he was looking for a boyfriend. I was dating a couple guys, and Joseph just ended a fling with a weird, psycho guy who stalked him. The relationship was really sexual right away." They told each other about sexual fantasies and about exotic and unusual encounters like three-ways in their pasts.

"Joseph was a little more experienced than me," Jason says, "but it was mostly because he's got a couple years on me and has been around the block a couple more times. I'd had three-way sex with a couple twice before Joseph and I met, but I still fantasized about doing it again, and about having group sex, and a lot of other things. I know that some fantasies are best if you just use them for talking dirty and for your own jerk-off fantasies because the reality can be really different than the fantasy. I was worried at the beginning of our relationship that he'd think I was telling him he's not enough for me if I shared fantasies. But I quickly learned that he's way more mature than that and I know that he knows that my desire for sex with him and a third person had nothing to do with how much I think he's worth to me. Plus, he was into the idea too, before we even discussed it."

After about two years of living together and three years of total sexual exclusivity, Joseph and Jason invited a third guy into their bedroom. Says Joseph, "We had lots of discussions about this before we agreed to do it, and we both decided we didn't want to end up like a couple I know who are really only having sex together when there's a third guy with them." Joseph describes the encounter as being "tentative," that the third guy mostly watched while Jason and Joseph had sex. "It was really exciting," said Jason, "and I wanted to do it again, and touch the other guy and have him touch us, and watch him with Joey and have Joey watch me with him."

Their discussions about three-ways continued to evolve until they came up with a few rules. The first rule was that neither Jason nor Joseph would ever have any kind of sexual contact with a third unless they were together. They were not free to have sex with other guys individually, and they were not permitted to bring a third home without checking with each other first. And they both have to find the third guy attractive. If ever they meet a guy who just wants Joseph or Jason but not both, they say "no thanks" and move on. A few of the guys they've invited over have come over again, but for the most part their three-way partners are one-time-only sex partners. "No crushes that way," explains Joseph. And the sex is always safe.

"Sometimes we go for a long stretch where we don't invite a third over, and sometimes it happens once every other week," says Jason. "It's been really liberating to know that I don't ever have to wonder about Joseph's affections. I can watch him having sex and know that it's just sex, and that his heart belongs to me."

This type of relationship relies on the emotional primacy of one long-term partner and keeping sexual encounters with anyone else a carefully circumscribed activity.

Open Relationships: Thom and Daniel

Thom, 41, and Daniel, 37, met online nine years ago. "We were both new to online hookups," says Thom, "but we both had pretty wild pasts. We started out as a one-night stand, and as soon as I came home from his place I called him up and asked him if he wanted to fuck again that weekend. He said yes, and we met like that—every few days or once a week—for about six months."

Daniel was apprehensive about getting into a relationship.

Though Thom was eager to have an LTR, he figured he could wait a bit. "Besides," Thom says, "I knew that Dan was fucking other guys too. It was fine by me—we weren't really dating yet. I've never been particularly jealous. I just wanted to know if he liked me. I asked him if he did, and he said he thought he was falling in love with me, but that he still liked having sex with other guys. Perfect! I thought, because I did too.

"We started dating and moved in together after dating for about a year and a half. I told him right away that I was fine with an open relationship, so long as he proved to me that he thought that sex with other guys was just for fun and not something he needed, and that it would always be safe sex only," Thom says. "So he gave up all other guys for six months. He didn't meet any other guys for sex until I told him I was OK with it. But I made him promise that he couldn't have full-on affairs, just one-time-only sex. And never in our house."

"I was the instigator in this," says Daniel. "I admit that. And at first I wasn't sure if it was going to ruin our relationship or not, but I figured that since I always wanted an open relationship, I wanted to be with a guy who was OK with that too. At first, after Thom gave me permission to have sex with other guys, I felt kind of guilty about it, because he wasn't going after other guys on his own. So it was 'don't ask, don't tell' for a while."

Both men felt they had satisfying sexual encounters with one another at home, and eventually Thom started asking Daniel about his hookups with other guys. "It really turned me on," says Thom. "It spiced up our sex at home, and then it got me excited about meeting other guys occasionally too. We've had sex with a third every now and then, and we tell each other our stories about the guys we've fucked around with alone too. It took some negotiating, but I'm glad we have this arrangement. We never feel restricted by one another, but we always come home together."

This open relationship also rests on the emotional primacy of one partner, and all other pairings are subordinate to that commitment.

The Three of Them Are a Couple: Greg, Mario, and Edgar

Greg, 35, and Mario, 32, had been dating for four years when they met Edgar, 26, at a rock concert. They talked with him all night and made plans to hang out together at a future date. One night they invited him to their house, and all three men had sex together. Edgar moved in three months later. Now all three are in a committed, polyamorous relationship.

"Mario and I had been having a great relationship," says Greg. "There was nothing wrong with it. But when we met Edgar, we both were immediately drawn to him. We had a great night bringing him home and all fucking each other for hours, so we asked him to stay the night. He slept between us the first night, and something about it felt so right for us."

Mario explains that it wasn't all smooth sailing at the beginning of their triad: "Both Greg and I were a little jealous about Edgar, but we both thought he was smart, hot, and such a sweet guy. As soon as we told each other how we felt about him—and that we still were in love with each other, we started thinking about inviting him to be part of our relationship. We didn't want a houseboy, and we didn't just want someone to fuck around with, so we asked him about it and he was interested. For a while, we all agreed not to have sex unless all three were there. It sort of set the ground rules about outside sexual activity—it's strictly not allowed."

"I loved the idea. I never thought there was a limit on the

number of people you could fall in love with," says Edgar. "I've been with Greg and Mario for two years, and it's been totally wonderful. But it's definitely different than being in a couple. There are two people's full personalities that you have to deal with. We have arguments and we have hot make-up sex, and we had to get a bigger bed to accommodate everyone—we switch off being in the middle. But we have a wonderful time, and I can't ever imagine my life without the two of them."

Successful Nonmonogamy

The common denominator for couples who are involved in successful and responsible nonmonogamous relationships is open, honest communication. Both (or all three) partners have to agree to set boundaries based on their level of comfort with sex with more than one person or sex outside of the relationship—and they have to agree to stick to the rules they've set. Rules can include conditions like, "we only do this on vacation," or "we only fool around with people we don't know." Negotiating the sexual contract between partners should take place over the course of many in-depth conversations until there's an agreement about acceptable behavior. Partners must make sure that neither one of them is simply caving in to the will of the other, and that neither one is pushing the other too hard toward agreement.

If you're in a nonmonogamous relationship, how do you know if someone is cheating? It's pretty simple: Cheating in a nonmonogamous relationship is when either partner strays from the contract he has made with his partner. Break the rules, and you've cheated. The difficult part is imagining all the scenarios you might be involved in so that your rules reflect the reality of your sexual appetites, your commitment to a partner, and your ability to adhere to a sexual contract.

How a Three-way Can Turn into a No-way

This cautionary tale is from the perspective of the third guy—the guy who was invited into a three-way that, because of a lack of communication between the partners, turned sour. Jon, 28, a writer in Los Angeles, describes his first three-way experience: "To find two other guys who were into me and into each other and generally amenable to a three-way was a tall order. So when I met this couple—let's call them Akbar and Jeff—I figured I'd found a shortcut to achieving my fantasy. The couple seemed cool enough. We met at a club and went back to their place. Things got hot and heavy pretty quickly. Akbar got up to leave the room, and Jeff stopped kissing me. He told me that he didn't want Akbar to think that he was fooling around behind his back— which I thought was hilarious since they'd both taken my pants halfway off already. It was a quickie lesson in how different guys define commitment differently.

"So Akbar came back and we all started fooling around again. Then Jeff went to the bathroom, and Akbar jumped me and started telling me that Jeff was too shy to say so but that I should fuck Akbar. 'He won't admit it, but he doesn't want to bottom, so you'd better just top me.' That was fine with me. Akbar had a great ass. Then he said, 'Oh, and he doesn't like to see me kissing other guys,' and then he planted one on my mouth just as Jeff was walking back into the room. Oops. They started fighting and I ended up walking home right after that with a total hard-on."

Jon was turned on by the spontaneity of the pickup, but Akbar and Jeff hadn't fully worked out a scheme for having sex with a third—and they went too far with Jon before telling him the terms of their poorly conceived (because they didn't agree) contract with each other. Sounds like a lot of rules and boundaries and hang-ups? Perhaps. Yes, hot sex is supposed to be thrilling and spontaneous, but if you're playing with both a partner and other people, you have to pay special attention to the conditions your partner sets with you. Otherwise, you're cheating.

Putting Yourself Back on the Market

Cruising for sex may have been second nature when you were single. Getting laid may have come easy, and perhaps you had a little black book of phone numbers for guys who were at your beck and call. But then you met a guy, fell in love, and you shacked up with him sometime during the first Bush administration for some hot monogamy. Now you're single again and looking to (re)sow some wild oats. You want to make the transition from having the same piece of meat once a month to dining out (hopefully) more than once a week.

Getting back out there can be a daunting task. The search for a new love—or maybe just a little afternoon delight—can be terrifying, but with a winning plan for reenergizing your sexuality, you'll be surprised how quickly you put the snap back in your turtle. There's no one right way to get your game back, but the following sections will help you decide what you're after and provide helpful tips on how to achieve your goals.

Decide if You're interested in Fucking or Dating

Yes, there's a difference between fucking and dating. Dating, of course, means meeting men socially for the possibility of a romantic relationship, and it's distinct from fucking primarily because of the mutual acknowledgement that there's an emotional attraction between the two of you as well as a physical one. Guys who are just coming out or who are returning to eligibility after a long-term monogamous relationship may be itching to get back in the saddle (or stirrups or sling) and to get to know lots of guys on a purely carnal level. It's a natural impulse, especially if the sexual spark had gone out of the former LTR. But as soon as you mix dating with sleeping with more than one guy, then you're fucking, and it's a different scenario. It's something you should be clear about with the guys who think you're dating them.

If you're having sex with some guys while you're dating others (who assume, rightly or wrongly, that you're not fucking anyone else), you're not playing fair, and you're not ready for dating. Maybe you're going through your slutty phase. Maybe you're really not ready for dating—that's totally OK. Just allow yourself the time to decide what you're interested in. But don't lead on a steady date by giving him the impression that he's the only one you're sleeping with.

If you do decide to become boyfriends, that means you've made an agreement to sexual exclusivity, unless you live on a commune or you're polyamorous, or it's an open relationship or there's a third person in your "couple." There are lots of variations to modern pairing up, of course, and you should feel unashamed to explore your sexual freedom however you like—but if you do it by fucking other guys and not telling your new boyfriend, then you're a louse. And that's nothing to be proud of.

Realize That the Search is Hard Work

Whether you're dating or fucking, meeting guys of like minds takes some work. It can be fun, exciting work, but it will be work. Dustin, 34, a furniture designer in Pittsburgh, just recently got out of a seven-year relationship. He's handsome and successful, but Dustin had never really dated. He met his ex just before he came out and had been with him ever since. Some other guys were interested in Dustin, but they knew that he was faithful to his partner. When his relationship ended, he very quickly got upset that his fantasies of having guys clamoring for him weren't coming true. "I wasn't really ready for the reality of being out there again. I mean, my relationship had run its course, but I think I had turned off parts of myself because I thought I didn't need them anymore."

Dustin had totally forgotten how to flirt. His seduction muscles had atrophied. "I mean, I knew what it looked like to score—I'm not a total hermit. But I was way out of practice. We were never really in gay bars all that much," he explains, "so I forgot what it feels like to go up to a guy and talk to him or ask him out."

He did eventually decide, with cajoling from some friends, to go out and socialize again following a self-imposed exile of four months after he split from his ex. "The first time I went out on the prowl was to a fund-raiser party, but I was a little shell-shocked. I was handling it OK until I confessed to a friend that I thought a guy at the other end of the host bar was cute. My friend started pushing me toward him, slowly at first, then, like, literally pushing me. There was nothing subtle about it. I was so embarrassed and it definitely showed! But I swallowed my pride anyway and said hi. It wasn't exactly smooth sailing the first time, but we ended up talking for a bit. He wasn't right for me, but I'd never have known if I hadn't introduced myself."

Dustin made it a personal goal to meet more eligible guys. The first few months were sort of dry until he reacquainted himself with the places in Pittsburgh where guys he was interested in liked to hang out. "I'd only gone to places like bars and clubs with my ex as a couple, so it was tough to know what to do at those places when I was not there with my boyfriend. Eventually I stopped going with friends every time, so I could be OK talking with guys. It's not easy meeting people, but it's still fun. I'm getting a little smoother when it comes to small talk too."

Get Reacquainted With Yourself

Yeah, it sounds kind of self-helpy, but you really need to get in touch with the kind of stuff you like to do and the kind of person you are as an individual when you're coming out of coupledom. In long-term relationships most people tend to do some of the activities they like to do, some of what their partners like to do, and some stuff they've discovered together that they only really enjoy doing as a couple. Couples develop joint habits, routines, and hobbies. When you're no longer a part of a couple and you're no longer interested in the activities that appealed to both of you, you might have to reacquaint yourself with your own interests.

Dustin gave up a favorite sport when he was with his ex-boyfriend, and he's just getting back into the swing now. "When I was single, I used to golf at least twice a month. When I was with my ex, I never really got the chance much. It's not like he didn't want me to golf. He even tried it a few times. But really, his heart wasn't in it. I'd go occasionally with a friend for a while, but since we both worked such long hours for a year or two, I let that interest go by the wayside so that we could have time together to do stuff we both enjoyed." Dustin recently dusted off his clubs for the first time in five years. "I was a little rusty, so I decided to start off at a driving range, then I got into playing nine holes with a beginner golfer friend—teaching him a little bit. The second time I was at one course, the cutest guy came up and said hi at the pro shop. He even offered to give me a few pointers. Then I gave him a few."

There's a sexual component to this personal reacquaintance activity as well. Emil, 30, a film director in New York, was in a relationship for three years with a rather vanilla guy—sexually speaking. "I'm totally into leather play and a little light S/M, but my boyfriend would have none of it. He had a great body and we had great sex, but we never really explored my limits like I wanted to. Whenever I asked my boyfriend to try out something new, like toys or leather harnesses or role-play, he would be adamantly opposed. I'm single again now, and I've been able to explore and to do a lot more sexually with this guy I met through a friend. This new guy is into a whole variety of things and he's not afraid to try something—even if he decides he doesn't like it."

Come Out Again—as Single

Amateur matchmakers can be just the ticket to finding eligible guys. Friends, coworkers, and even casual acquaintances (like, say, the chatty woman who works at the post office) can help set you up with dates. If you're newly single, many of your casual friends and coworkers may not know you're solo yet, so make sure you come out to them—as single. Tell them that you're putting yourself back on the market and you'd like to meet new guys. Take off your wedding/commitment ceremony band, take those vacation photos of you and your ex off your desk, change your answering machine so that only *your* voice and name greets callers, and take his picture off the wall and out of your wallet. Start fresh.

Who knows you better than your friends? Let them play the

yenta and help them help you meet some new men. If you're comfortable talking about sex with your friends (and why wouldn't you be?) tell them you're dying for a hot hookup—if scoring is on your mind. Or tell them that you'd like to meet some guys to date.

X Out the Ex

No matter how hard he dumped you or how long it's taken you to get over his sorry ass, no new guy wants to hear about how rotten your ex was—unless the guy is your therapist. (And your therapist gets about a hundred and fifty really good reasons an hour to want to listen.) The guy you asked out to dinner for a first date doesn't want to hear about how your ex never really liked your dog, and the trick you blew in the steam room of your gym definitely doesn't want to hear about your ex's bad habit of picking his nose. Whining about your ex is never, ever, sexy, and it can make you look like damaged goods. Guys who seek out other guys who are emotionally damaged because they think they'll make perfect boyfriend material are often damaged goods themselves. You shouldn't be with guys who want to fix you. And, truthfully, they shouldn't be allowed to have boyfriends.

On the other hand, if your ex is a friend now and he comes over on Sundays for bagels and the Sunday paper and you water each other's plants when you're out of town, your ex might be screwing up your prospects for future love interests. This might be the case even if his motivations appear benevolent. Staying friends with an ex is a quick and easy way to scare off eligible guys. "My ex, Tom, lived with his ex when we met," says Arleigh, 28, an associate professor at a university in Los Angeles. "He assured me that they had a platonic relationship now, and that they didn't like the idea of sex with each other. I was apprehensive, and I never totally got over the idea that they were now best friends and they might have a kind of intimacy that I'd never get with Tom. I was just the boyfriend, but Tom's ex was the ex *and* the best friend *and* the roommate. It bothered me throughout our relationship, and it always seemed to me that his ex was a little jealous of me too. I never totally got over it, and it didn't end well."

Cutting ties with your ex is a better way to make room for a future relationship. This doesn't mean that you have to eliminate all contact with your former boyfriend, especially if you share custody of the kids, or a business, or property. But make sure that being friendly with your ex leaves plenty of room for relationships with other guys.

Putting Yourself in the Right Place

Guys are not simply going to flock to you if you stay at home on Saturday nights. Some eligible guys probably wrote you off long ago as committed, so you're now not even a blip on their radar. It's not their fault for thinking you're unavailable—it's been a while since you were in circulation. You need to draw some amorous attention your way by putting yourself in the path of the kinds of guys who turn your crank. They're not going to come find you if they don't know to start looking.

You need to drop the TV remote, put down the computer mouse, and look for things to do. If you like music and the nightlife, then head out to the clubs. If you enjoy working out or exercise, then get to the gym—or go on a hike or take a yoga class or join a gay softball team. There are gay political clubs and gay nudist groups and gay cafés and gay cooking classes. Go to your local LGBT center and see what kinds of activities they list on their community boards. Join a book club at your local gay bookstore. Donate some of your time to a gay philanthropic organization. You've heard all these suggestions before, right? (Join a cooking class! Volunteer!) Well, the reason that guys like me keep suggesting them is that, even when we're *not* looking for playmates and boyfriends, we meet lots of guys at these types of events and activities.

Go where the boys are. If you're in a big city, go shopping or out for lunch in your gay ghetto. (By the way, hanging out in the gay ghetto occasionally doesn't mean that you have to turn your life all-gay-all-the-time. You won't instantly become a stereotype unless you choose to work at it.) But putting yourself in the midst of other gay men makes sense if you're interested in meeting new guys who like guys.

Retail Therapy

OK, not all gay men like to shop. The point of a little retail therapy isn't that you'll feel better about being single simply by buying some cashmere. If only it were so easy.... And I'm not suggesting that you max out your credit cards for that "charge it!" endorphin boost. What I'm suggesting is that by updating your wardrobe—an activity often ignored when you're nesting in an LTR—getting a new haircut, and maybe giving your exterior a nice buff-'n'-polish, you can instantly increase your confidence. And we all know confidence is attractive. Plus, the new clothes and the new haircut might look a little more flash than the duds and coif you're sporting now. By ditching that old Mickey Mouse sweatshirt your ex gave you years ago—and by giving to charity any clothes of his that he *still* has not retrieved from your closet—you're telling yourself that you're not hanging on to the past. Even more importantly, you're showing yourself and the world that you're ready to move on into the future. Try it—it's cathartic!

Go Online

If you've been in a relationship and all you've really done online in the past few years is look at dirty pictures of young, muscled guys poking other young, hot guys, then there's a whole world of online activity you've got to catch up on. There's a wide variety of online activities specifically geared to gay men. There's online dating, hooking up, and a half-and-half hybrid. Online dating is less sordid than it used to be. There are now sites where you post a profile about yourself and your interests and post a fully clothed photo. Then you search the site for other interesting online profiles. You can exchange e-mails with like-minded guys who are looking for dates in your area, and perhaps you can go out on a date with one or several guys. (Go on, champ—get out there!)

Then there's hooking up. The sites and chat rooms where guys go to hook up make no pretense about romance or about finding an LTR or a partner. They clearly indicate that the point of their service is to help you find hot guys in your area who are looking for sex so you can hook up and fuck.

The third variety of online activity is a mix between the two types of services, where guys can search for winging and dinging, or just sixty-nining. On their profiles at these sites, guys can mark a box (*so* ninth-grade study hall!) to indicate whether they're look-ing for love or lust. If you're interested in venturing into the cyber-world for the purpose of meeting men, you should know which sites offer what services. Most Web dating sites offer inexpensive or free trial periods. Try out a few different sites rather than put-ting all your eggs in one basket. This will allow you to get a sense for what men on a given site are looking for, and it will keep you from being too surprised when you discover that the guys on *www.homofuckpigs.com* aren't really looking for LTRs and "watching sunsets and taking long drives in the country"—unless they also add "and fucking like wild boars when we get there."

Well, which is it? It's an important distinction and it could determine the quality of the sex you have in the future. As we've learned, it can be fun to act like a slut sometimes or to revisit your slutty phase, but your being an *actual* slut is not particularly attractive to eligible guys. Studs, on the other hand, get all the action they can handle—but they do it while respecting the guys they're sleeping with. We need more men who know what they're doing in bed. Still, we'd rather have more studs than sluts in the world. Here's a little rundown, based on the previous chapters, on the distinctions between studs and sluts.

A slut will settle for anyone.
A stud won't go home with someone if he's not really interested in him.

A slut will cheat on a boyfriend.
A stud will invite you to play with him and his boyfriend.

A slut doesn't know the meaning of the word no.
A stud takes no for an answer.

A slut ends the night with a bunch of wadded-up phone numbers in his pocket, unsure of which guy to call.
A stud ends the night with his phone number programmed in someone else's phone.

A slut will forget your name and confuse you with your roommate.
A stud will remember your name, where you met, and that special spot on your neck that drives you wild.

A slut will perform his sexual repertoire on you, regardless of how well it's working.
A stud listens to your responses to his moves and works his mojo accordingly.

A slut sleeps with guys because he can.
A stud sleeps with a guy because he's attracted to him.

ARE YOU A STUD OR A SLUT?

A slut has a trail of guys who will tell you how hung and talented he is.
A stud has tons of friends who will tell you what a great guy he is.

A slut prefers to get some, safe or not.
A stud enjoys sex but won't compromise by having unsafe sex.

A slut never graduates from the slutty phase.
A stud did the slutty phase, learned from it, and matured.

A slut says "let's get together" but doesn't really mean it.
A stud says "let's get together" and will give you a time and a date and a reason to do it.

A slut grabs your package.
A stud grabs your attention with his confidence.

A slut licks before he looks.
A stud looks before he jumps into bed.

A slut will lead a guy on if it means more sex.
A stud will never lead a guy on if he's not interested in dating him.

A slut will fuck his friends.
A stud keeps fuck buddies and friends separate.

A slut won't tell you he's only looking for a no-strings-attached arrangement.
A stud will always be honest and up-front about his motives.

GLOSSARY

BDSM—sex play involving any of the aspects of bondage/discipline, dominance/submission, or sadism/masochism

cottaging—British slang for casual, often anonymous sexual activity between men in public bathrooms

doggie style—the quintessential rear-entry anal sex position where the bottom gets on his hands and knees (like a dog) and the top penetrates him from behind

frottage—non-penetrative sex, also known as "dry humping"

hate-fuck—vigorous sexual activity with a person you do not like or are angry with, yet whom you find attractive

high heels—anal sex position where the bottom lies on his back with his legs spread or his knees tucked to his chest. The top lies on the bottom or kneels in front of him with the bottom's ankles in his hands. This allows for very deep penetration.

GLOSSARY

homonomics—the market forces of gay dating, determined by the supply of fuckable gay men and the demand for sex

interfemoral intercourse—nonpenetrative sex in which the top puts his lubed dick between the thighs of the bottom and makes thrusting / fucking motions until he climaxes

Lucky Pierre—the man in a ménage à trois who is simultaneously penetrating one man and being penetrated by another

over-the-shoulder syndrome—a condition in which a potential hookup, during a conversation with you, keeps looking over your shoulder for other eligible men in the room

Princeton belly rub—frottage technique where one man lies on top of another and they rub their cocks together to orgasm

slutty phase—natural developmental period in a gay man's life when he is nonmonogamous and very busy

tied off—using a cock ring, twine, leather strap, or other cord-like material tied loosely around the base of the penis and testicles to engorge the genitals, making them look larger. A favorite technique of go-go dancers

tweaking—high on drugs, typically crystal methamphetamine (also called tina, crystal meth, krank, tweak, ice), an intense stimulant with disinhibitory qualities.

ugly-hot—describes men who aren't conventionally good-looking but who are sexually appealing nonetheless (e.g., Harvey Keitel, Tommy Lee Jones, Humphrey Bogart)